The Spartan Life

SA WESTERMAN /4/.

The Spartan Life

Observations from the
Banks of the Red Cedar

By Scott Westerman

Associate Vice President for
Alumni Relations - Executive Director
Michigan State University Alumni Association

Published in 2010 by
Scott Westerman
East Lansing, Michigan
www.scottwesterman.com
ISBN: 978-0-578-05807-8

For Colleen

Who understands that working for
Michigan State University
is not a job, it's a lifestyle.

Table of Contents

Foreword

When Michigan State University opened its doors to students in 1857 as the Agricultural College of the State of Michigan, it comprised five faculty members, three buildings, 63 students, and a university president. The campus was predominantly undeveloped; both the academic and physical infrastructure needed to be built from the ground up. Further, the curriculum, focused on scientific agriculture, was new in higher education, as were the types of students admitted to the college. As part of an experiment, students at Michigan State University were recruited from the farming and working classes that had hitherto not been considered appropriate candidates for traditional higher education.

From these challenging roots, however, has sprung Michigan State University, a nationally and internationally ranked, research-intensive institution of higher education that graduates more than 10,000 students every year.

How did this experiment, which could just as easily have failed as succeeded, come to be Michigan State University?

In this book, Scott Westerman, a graduate of Michigan State, provides insight into how individuals can accomplish great works—to the benefit of companies and institutions as well as themselves—through positive attitudes and actions focused on a picture bigger than themselves. His ideas provide the basis for team building for the betterment of all. This same attitude drove MSU's earliest faculty and students to build a university from the bottom up, and it is the spirit that drives MSU to reach beyond its borders today to create a university prepared to engage with the world for the betterment of humanity.

MSU calls this approach to life and work TEAM MSU. Every position at our university—from the most Distinguished Professor to administrators and support staff—collaborates to make Michigan State the success that it is. The idea that "everyone connected to MSU makes MSU" arises from its roots in 1857, when everyone on campus did everything to move the university and its vision forward. Students performed three hours of manual labor every day; the president was also the farm manager; professors taught classes across disciplines. Their passion for making a difference in the nineteenth century drove them to embrace every challenge and conquer it. Today's Michigan State University rose from these values and continues to flourish by following these same principles.

Scott's ideas provide the basis for individuals to accomplish great things in their lives and in the world. As an integral part of TEAM MSU, he understands that success comes from a passion for excellence and the commitment to see that passion to fruition.

In his writings, he shows how these ideas are available to everyone. I am sure that countless people, both in and outside the academy, will benefit from reading Scott's work and putting his ideas into practice.

Lou Anna K. Simon
President
Michigan State University

Preface

I envision a life without limits.

It is something that my parents instilled in me from birth, my mentors have reinforced, and I have learned, first hand, throughout an existence that seems to be accelerating with the years.

In 1978, I heard my first Earl Nightingale tape. It was called Twenty Minutes That Can Change Your Life. It changed mine. Earl's focus on the power of your mind, how attitude is everything, and how "we become what we think about," was an inspiration.

I began to devour the works of Napoleon Hill, W. Clement Stone, Tom Hopkins and Denis Waitley. Later on; Tom Peters, Jim Collins, Seth Godin and Keith Ferrazzi became my virtual mentors.

I learned that happiness is something we choose. As Francesca Reigler said, "We either make our-selves miserable, or happy and strong. The amount of work is the same."

I also discovered the common trait of all truly great people:

They pay it forward.

In my own experience, giving is much more fun than receiving. And one of the best kept secrets about giving is this: When you give without the expectation of return, what you get back is exponential.

This collection began as a weekly email exercise. Each Sunday afternoon, I turn to the keyboard to find something inspirational to share with my MSUAA team. The Monday Motivator as it came to be known ended up with a wider distribution than I could have dreamed, with readers in 24 states and a dozen different countries.

Such is the magic of the Internet.

As the weeks progressed, I was humbled to learn that a few of these essays were finding their way beyond my small listserv and website. One day, Jennifer Decker, my able altar ego and executive associate said, "Why don't you put these in a book?".

So, for better or worse, here they are. Brief shots of inspiration collected from minds greater than my own, distilled into essays that I hope will, in turn, help you find more joy, more success and more opportunities to do what we Spartans do best;

Make the world a better place!

Scott Westerman
East Lansing, Michigan
December, 2010

What is a Spartan?

"A Spartan dreams of the future. But we do more than just dream. We actively participate in creating it."

I am often asked what it is that makes Michigan State University unique. In a world with thousands of excellent institutions of higher education, what is it that sets Spartans apart?

In the 37 years since I first set foot on her campus, I've had the opportunity to know many people who have benefited directly or indirectly from the MSU magic. I've learned that not everyone who graduates is a true Spartan. But anyone who truly want's to model the MSU spirit can become one.

Spartans emerge from the most modest of backgrounds and from the most prominent families. We represent every color of the rainbow and every corner of the globe. Our backgrounds are all uniquely ours, but our common connection is a quest for knowledge that can help us improve the world.

A Spartan reads the classics, creates art and studies the fundamental laws of the universe. We may make three point shots, swim faster and run further, but we know that a broad educational experience is a greater predictor of success than a one dimensional focus.

Spartans have known pain, disappointment and struggle. But we realize that only the hottest fire refines our resolve and defines our character. We make mistakes and suffer setbacks.

But Spartans learn from experience, get up when we stumble, and are ultimately victorious in any endeavor we undertake.

Spartans achieve, but remain humble. The greatest among us are defined, not by our position, but by our kindness, caring and humility

Spartans are catalysts for change. We seek clean, sustainable energy, just as we sought and created the agriculture that is feeding the world. We participate in the political process and welcome the opportunity to be servant-leaders.

Spartans are often passionate. We may sometimes protest in the intense tradition of our ancestors. In the end, we are collaborative. We strive for consensus and ultimately find solutions that benefit the greater good.

A Spartan believes that where we came from can give us perspective, but it's where we are going that makes all the difference.

A Spartan welcomes individuality. We know that if we discuss and debate from a place of diversity we are more likely to make the right decisions when we act as one.

Spartans have open minds and open hearts. We seek to understand, are slow to judge and quick to assist.

The philanthropic spirit of MSU's World Grant Mission is deeply imbedded in who we are. Spartans are among the first to offer a hand to those in need. And we devote our time, talent and treasure to create a margin of excellence that ensures, enriches and sustains our beloved Institution for future generations.

A Spartan always helps other Spartans, anytime, anywhere. The MSU bond transcends status, achievement and experience. It is a half million individual strands, woven tightly together into an unbreakable force that educates, inspires and enlightens everything it touches.

A Spartan never stops learning. We believe that knowledge is more than just power. It's the invisible fuel that nourishes our psyche, can solve any problem and leads to peace and understanding.

A Spartan dreams of the future. But we do more than just dream about it. We actively participate in creating it.

Spartans are all these things and more. Our dedication to the greater good is unmatched. Our determination is unbroken. Our compassion is legendary. And our common connection with Michigan State University sustains and strengthens us in everything we do.

We are proud, hardworking, inclusive, practical, bold, genuine, empowering and principled.

We are Spartans.

Life with a Purpose

"The purpose of life is life with a purpose" – Robert Byrne

Dave Isbell isn't your typical career counselor. As the guy who helps our mid-career MSU alumni reinvent themselves, Dave encourages his clients to spend a lot of time figuring out what makes them happy.

Science tells us that the longevital capacity of the human body is around 90 years. In the U.S. we typically live to age 78. There's a growing body of research that connects living longer to living with a purpose.

Dan Buettner has spent much of his life studying the factors that contribute to a long, productive life. Talking with NPR this week, Buettner suggests setting up "permanent nudges and defaults" to help keep you focused on the behaviors that contribute to longevity.

"For example," he told NPR's Weekend Edition Sunday host Liane Hansen, "In our financial lives, we know that financial security has a three-times greater impact on our happiness than just income alone, so setting up automatic savings plans, and buying insurance as opposed to buying a new thing. The newness effect of a new thing wears off in nine months to a year, but financial security can last a lifetime."

Both Dan and Dave would agree that where you choose to work and the friends you cultivate there make a big difference in how much you'll like your job. Isbell admonishes us to choose where you express your personal brand with care. And once you align it with a company, proactively making friends there is key.

Buettner recommends being the one that organizes Happy Hour.

That's exactly what my friends <u>Kat Cooper</u> and <u>Ryan</u> and <u>Jess</u> Knott do. As the energy behind the "<u>Lansing Happy Hour Club</u>," Kat, Ryan and Jess focus more on the relationships than on the liquid consumption that is typically associated with post-work bar conclaves. Colleen and I aren't big drinkers. But we look forward to visiting with the ever changing group of attendees every week.

LHHC attracts fascinating people who are doing interesting things. And since our quality of life is directly connected to the people who surround us, cultivating your social network is just as important as building a professional network.

Working with National Geographic and the National Council on Aging, Buettner identified four geographic areas where people are living the longest.

One key is celebrating longevity. In Sardinia, revering maturity is part of the culture. It has also been shown to have an impact on the next generation, where youth mortality is significantly lower than elsewhere in the world.

Okinawa has five times the number of centenarians and 1/6 the incidence of cardiovascular disease, compared to our American life. A plant based diet is a one dimension, but portion size is also a factor. Confucius recommended that we stop eating when we feel 20% full, since it takes a half an hour for that feeling to travel from our stomachs to our brains.

When all is said and done, it turns out that the most important contributor to a long life is having a reason to wake up in the morning.

Expressing a passion leads to other healthy behaviors. Passionate people are more likely to have regular physical activity and eat a diet that promotes health. And despite the perception that passion is all about activity, long life is directly connected to an ability to periodically slow down. Meditation can have just as much of an influence on your health as diet and exercise, when all three are combined.

This was brilliantly illustrated for me this morning when I ran into Bonnie Knutson at our gym. We're in the depths of a Michigan winter that makes you want to stay under those warm covers as long as you can. Not Bonnie. She's at our club several times a week, well before the workday starts and attacks her fitness program with a gusto that would challenge our most elite athletes. She does it because she want's to keep up with her grandkids.

And it shows. Earlier this year, she and her granddaughter rappelled down the side of the tallest building in town as part of a fundraiser. And at an age when most people would be slowing down, she still teaches one of the most popular classes at MSU's School of Hospitality Business. It's tough, and the students love it.

Bonnie's life is a continual adventure because she decided it would be. She inspires me to push myself in the gym and to continue to bracket my passions so I can know the joy she finds in living every day.

Take stock of your daily routine. Who do you associate with? How do you structure your days? What fuel are you putting into your marvelous machine? And what is your reason for getting up in the morning?

Whether it's the joys of deep friendship or concentrating on a passion that touches the core of you're being, living with a purpose can facilitate a portfolio of healthy behaviors.

These elements mix in a magical alchemy that can translate into a long... and exuberant life.

Learning from Michigan

"Speramus Meliora; Resurget Cineribus:
We Hope For Better Things;
It Shall Rise From the Ashes" – Detroit's Motto

On January 1, 2010, I became the new Head Servant for the Michigan State University Alumni Association. As I told friends about our move from New Mexico back to Michigan, the reactions have been, to use a popular phrase, "shock and awe".

"This is the perfect job for you," said many, "but why would you move back to Michigan?"

Aside from the Winter, which we largely avoided for three years in New Mexico, the conversations quickly turned to the state of the Michigan economy.

We can learn a lot from the Great Lakes State. A lot about how the mighty fall and how the strong survive. It's a good object lesson for leaders.

When good companies get in trouble its often due to a combination of five factors:
- They didn't have a Plan B
- They did not adapt
- They forgot about the customer
- They got greedy
- They didn't believe that something so big could fail

That's what happened in my home state. We depended too much on the auto industry. Even as competitors innovated, the perception was that we didn't. Driving in Detroit, where everyone owns an American made car, we were blind to the influx of foreign vehicles everywhere else across the country. Our workforce and company shareholders continued to demand a higher return for their investments of time and money, even as customers demanded more for theirs. Nobody could believe that the Big Three could ever truly be in real trouble.

Analysts could see this collapse coming a mile away, even as many Michiganians were stunned by the depth and breadth of the economic downturn in our State.

There will be those who argue that things like NAFTA and Tom Friedman's World-Is-Flat-isms were partly to blame. Whatever the outside contributors may have been, in the words of Clint Eastwood in "Heartbreak Ridge," our duty is to "Adapt and Overcome."

It's a hard lesson, but with my prodigal eyes, I can see that Michigan has learned from it.

Being a Green Blood, I love to use Michigan State University as an example of an organization that is doing a lot of things right in these uncertain times.

President Simon not only has a Plan B, but a Plan C, D, E, F and G. MSU has adapted, launching new educational initiatives in the Middle East and closer to home, investing just down the street in Detroit. MSU's Plan B included winning cutting edge government funding for the high tech research that will chart our future and maximizing the promise of renewable energy. MSU has redefined customer service on the student's terms, utilizing technology for everything from PDF delivery of college transcripts to enabling your student ID as a credit card. As a volunteer, and now as an employee, I've seen first hand how carefully money is "invested" (not spent) at MSU.

Yup, I'm biased, and there are probably some out there who have a different view, but I use my beloved University as an example of what we all need to do as we look forward to the new year.

- What's your Plan B? If you were to lose your job this week, what would you do? Have you built your network now, before you need it? Do you have 6-12 months worth of expenses in the bank?
- Are you anticipating how things might be done differently at your company, and are you working now to be the kind of person who can do it? What was your 2009 investment in self development?
- When is the last time you were in front of a customer, face to face? What did you learn from that encounter? Did you provide feedback to your boss?
- How can you offer more value for the money that the company is investing in you? What's hindering your personal productivity?
- Have you thought about how you would face failure as the learning experience it truly is? Are you learning from history so you don't have to repeat it?

My many friends who still live and work in Michigan have been thinking a LOT about these things lately. I'm sure that those who didn't have concrete goals in each of these areas before, have them now.

My writing mentor and long time journalist Susan Whitall reminded me of one of Berry Gordy, Jr.'s great maxims as to why his Motown record label could be such a feisty competitor among the big record boys in New York and LA. Gordy firmly believes that Motown couldn't have happened anywhere else but Detroit, where people have been weathering challenges for decades. "Putting chains on the tires, brushing the snow off, we had to do a day's work, just to get to work!" Gordy told Susan last year. "That gave us an advantage over the competition, they were soft!"

That's still true. There's a pioneer work ethic that built our great State. And it can re-emerge, stronger, wiser and better than before.

Couple tenacity with a game plan in your life, and eventual victory is assured.

The Basics

"Success is neither magical nor mysterious.
Success is the natural consequence of consistently applying
the basic fundamentals." – Jim Rohn

I recently met a retired medical man. He was in his 80s and still vigorous, working as a consultant to other medical people who wanted to sell their practices and retire. He told me of an encounter between seller and prospect. The prospect, whom I am certain was well trained and fully licensed, appeared in a t-shirt, shorts and flip-flops. He had the money and liked the price.

But the owner balked. "Write me a business plan."

In a week the prospective buyer returned. His plan was scribbled on a legal pad.

No sale.

My medical friend concluded his story with this observation: "Why would you hand over the patients you love, let alone a job to someone who was not as committed, as prepared and as professional as you were?"

Again and again, I've found that the reason so many people have trouble finding a good gig, earning a great performance review and growing in esteem and happiness is because so few people have learned the basics.

So let's get down to basics.

- Speak well: The English playwright and poet, Ben Johnson, wrote, "Talking and eloquence are not the same: to speak, and to speak well, are two things." Use proper grammar. Have a vocabulary of more than 250 words. Be respectful in tone.

- Dress well: In many places, business casual has devolved to the uniform our unlucky medical suitor wore. Dress like the professional you hope to be. Your clothes should be tailored to fit and be clean and pressed. Wear conservative shoes and make sure they are polished.

- Prepare: Find out everything you can about the job you seek, the company where you hope to work, and the person who is making the hiring decision. You will very likely be asked, "So... What do you know about our firm?" Dream up some solutions to the challenges you see the company facing. Bosses like to hire people that help them solve problems.

- Customize your personal brand: The biggest waste of time, trees and Internet bandwidth is blasting out a generic resume. Describe how your past experience relates to the specific gig you seek. Select references who can speak to how well you might perform in that particular environment. Do NOT write a Job Objective statement. Everyone knows that you want to "secure a strong position as a (fill in the blank) with a cutting edge (the type of work the company does) firm." And be careful how you express yourself on the Internet. If a Google search reveals how many times you puked at your last fraternity party, that may impact perceptions.

- Listen: "If speaking is silver, then listening is gold." This Turkish proverb says it all. Among the pontifications you hear and questions you are asked along the way, you'll get a pretty good picture of what the company is looking for and the character of its leadership. If you've done your homework, your answers to the interviewer's queries will come naturally. By the way, it's ok to say, "I don't know," if you don't know.

- Be confident but humble: There's a thin line between sounding like you know what you're doing and sounding like a know-it-all.

- Be grateful: These people were kind enough to give you their time. They didn't have to. Appreciate that and show it.

- Follow up and follow through: Send a thank you note that reiterates your excitement about the job and hits at least one qualification you wanted to amplify. Find ways to keep in contact without coming across as too pushy.

- Don't burn bridges: I remember visiting my congresswoman's office when we lived in Illinois. I witnessed her telling a colleague on the other side of the isle that she couldn't support his bill. She did it in a way that would have made me send her flowers, even if I disagreed with her. Don't get angry if the HR department doesn't get back to you. Companies have a way of delaying and re-thinking. It took me three months after an interview before my future boss called me back with an offer.

These 9 points also apply to growing your career in your current role. Good communication, appropriate attire, preparation and performance inevitably lead to good things both inside and outside of the office.

What is Success?

What is the mark of a successful person? Visit the self help section of any bookstore and you'll see a wagon load of opinion on that topic. Here's one example from a guy named Pinyo, a 34 year old investment guru.

Successful people:

- Know what they want
- Don't just think, they act
- Have an insatiable hunger for knowledge
- Are curious and not afraid to experiment
- Build their networks
- Are passionate about what they do
- Are persistent and patient

That's a good start.

I would add that successful people:

- Are good listeners
- Fail often, but get back up and try again
- Have a positive attitude about life
- Love to teach others how to be successful
- Pay it forward by contributing to causes that are important to them
- Want to make the world a better place

Based on these definitions, many who our tabloid society may call successful don't fill the bill.

I used to believe that being a success meant displaying the outward signs of affluence. Then I learned about people like Dave Packard (The Hewlett / Packard Dave Packard), who helped create silicon valley, generated billions of dollars of shareholder value, was loved by his employees and his neighbors, but lived simply and wanted his head stone to say "David Packard – Farmer".

We read about the so-called successful people who move from marriage to marriage, who struggle as parents, and are so self focused that there is little room "between the I's".

And then we read about Ghandi and Mother Theresa who suffered greatly but consistently said things like, "The miracle is not that we do the work, but that we are happy to do it."

As I become more seasoned, it seems to me that the true definition of success is:

Happiness.

If you reread the list of traits, above, you will see that every one probably applies to a happy person you know.

One of the happiest people I met this year was a porter at the Omni Hotel in Jacksonville, Florida. He wouldn't make the Forbes list that Bill Gates is on. He told me that at age 64, he's making less than $20.00 per hour, but as we rode the elevator from my high perch to the lobby, he exuded joy.

He loves living in a place where he can see the ocean every day. He maintains his health by taking long walks. He loves to read.

He travels when he feels like it (almost always by train, he was once an Amtrak porter). He volunteers on Saturday mornings at the local homeless shelter. "A buddy in every county," he says about his network of good friend across the country. He loves his job.

"I reckon that I'm a happier man than about 90% of the people in the world," he told me. "If I can rub some of that off on a guest or two each day, it's a good day."

My philosophical mentor, Denis Waitley, believes that it's ok to put lots of points on the board, but at the end of the day, it isn't the money that will make you truly happy.

"Happiness cannot be traveled to, owned, earned, worn or consumed," he says. "Happiness is the spiritual experience of living every minute with love, grace and gratitude."

So when you ponder your goals and objectives, think seriously about what makes YOU happy? What's standing between you and that happiness right now? What steps will you take next year to bring more happiness into your life? How can you live every minute with love, grace and gratitude?

Life is short. Choose happiness!

The Walk On

Marcel Mayberry is a good judge of character. The proprietor of T-Styles, the barber shop in the basement of the MSU Union has seen a lot of people come and go. So when he tells me that Brandon Chambers is the real deal, I am interested.

It's a Thursday afternoon, and I'm sitting in Marcel's chair as he does his best with my ever thinning dome.

"This guy hangs out across the hall in the computer center. He's trying to make his football dream come true. First kid in his family to go to college. Came here on a leadership scholarship. He's not a one dimensional athlete. He's someone you'd be proud to put up in front of a crowd and say, 'This guy is a real Spartan.'"

He looked out of his window toward what used to be the billiard room. It's now filled with rows and rows of computers, targeting kids with budgets that prioritize food and credit hours above technology. Near the doorway sat an intense African-American, focusing on a computer screen. It seemed like everyone else in the room had their headphones on. Brandon didn't.

"That's him. He's a walk-on."

That said it all.

- Walk-ons choose the institution, even if the institution didn't initially choose them.
- Walk-ons have to try harder, be better and wait longer.
- Walk-ons must prove the dictionary definition of "student athlete". They have to show that they have the brains to match the brawn.
- Walk-ons are the first to the weight room, the first to the track and the first to the library. They are often the last to leave.
- The odds are stacked against them, so walk-ons learn about tenacity, mental toughness and internalizing the dream in a way that scholarship winners don't.

MSU's Javon Ringer was a walk-on. He's playing in the NFL.

My co-worker, Tim Bograkos was a walk-on. MSU's legendary basketball coach, Tom Izzo, named an award after him.

"You have to put your ego aside and work for the good of the program," Tim says. He doesn't even mention that his last second shot came at just the right time to propel the Spartans further up the NCAA ziggurat. Walk-ons are humble.

I spent a half an hour with Brandon Chambers that day. His faith is strong. He is family focused. He is refreshingly open about his hopes, dreams and fears. He spends what little free time he has serving the homeless in center-city Detroit and gives inspirational talks to kids about making the right choices.

He is an advertising major at my beloved College of Com Arts. Whether or not his walk-on dream comes true, I can sense that Brandon is already a winner.

Re-read those descriptions of the traits a walk-on. How many of those behaviors do you model right now?

In my leadership career, some of the best people I've hired came to me after I had initially passed on what I read in their resumes. They understood the old adage that there is not a lot of competition on the extra mile.

Tiare Romero and Diane Villegas are two examples. For many years they worked in the shadows, able foot soldiers who helped make their supervisors look good. My bosses had not pictured them as superstars. But they both knew they could be.

They stepped forward and asked for the shot. When they got their opportunity, they made the most of it. Diane and Tiare helped our team build an attitude...An attitude that we could achieve excellence, even when others said we couldn't.

They carried that attitude with them when they spread their wings and grew into larger roles with more responsibility.

So when I look for a key player to take us beyond the conventional and into the exceptional...

Give me a walk-on.

Commitment

If you've ever experienced the precursor symptoms to a root canal, you know how Colleen felt one uncomfortable Spring weekend. By Saturday afternoon, we were calling around to see if we could find a dentist who could bring The Queen down from the ceiling.

A friend recommended Dan Gulick. He and his wife met in dental school and have shared a practice together for 27 years. Dan is a committed family man. He was watching his son play baseball far away, but took our call anyway and suggested we contact Kyle.

Long story short, we ended up meeting her at her office on Sunday morning. She spent four hours of her Mother's Day making Colleen better.

We live in a world where people are constantly jumping to the new shiny thing. People increasingly choose careers that suit a nine to five schedule. Gen Y kids are said to switch jobs in a heartbeat, if it doesn't fit their lifestyle. We all know about the uncomfortably high divorce rate.

It's easily forgotten that the single most important behavior that leads to achievement is commitment.

My mentor, Jim Collins of *Good to Great* fame, writes, "The kind of commitment I find among the best performers across virtually every field is a single-minded passion for what they do, an unwavering desire for excellence in the way they think and the way they work. Genuine confidence is what launches you out of bed in the morning, and through your day with a spring in your step."

Jim speaks as much to my continuing sermon about doing what you love, and loving what you do. But his words remind us that the habit of excellence is based on the foundation of commitment.

Stan Stein, Executive Vice President at Weber Shandwick, the powerhouse PR firm that specializes in advising Fortune 50 companies, tells a story about how a Natural Science class at Michigan State University stood in the way of his matriculation. After receiving a failing grade on his first exam, he did what most students don't do.

He approached his professor for help.

Teachers recognize and reward commitment, and Stan's encouraged him to attend all three sections of the class. The professor offered to stay 30 minutes after each class to answer Stan's questions. The 2010 MSU Communications Arts and Sciences Distinguished Alumnus said he didn't get a four point, but he passed the course. He's been committed to excellence ever since.

In the elite world of high performance you always need to be on your A-game. The difference be-tween leading the field and getting stuck in the pack is the work you're willing to do in the extra mile.

- Commitment is taking the time to figure out what happiness really means.
- Commitment is due diligence before decision.
- Commitment is an inoculation against distraction.
- Commitment on both sides is the steel that forges a lasting relationship.
- Commitment refines and transforms dreams as they come closer to reality.
- Commitment is malleable but unbreakable.
- Commitment overcomes fear.
- Commitment repels negativity.
- Commitment is the fuel that recharges energy.

How many of these definitions fit your outlook, your goals, your behavior?

My boss at MSU Advancement, Bob Groves, likes to put it another way, "To the chicken, a ham and eggs breakfast requires only a small contribution, but to the pig, a total commitment is required!"

When NBA Hall of Famer Ervin Johnson used to come by WVIC in the days when we were both in East Lansing, it was clear, even then, that Magic was focused. "I was able to see what I wanted to do," he wrote later, "I could see the opportunity, even when others could not. I stay committed to doing it and doing it well, no matter what."

We didn't know Dr. Kyle Gulick before this weekend. But we will tell everyone we know that she and her husband are the best dentists in town.

Her ninth grade passion for dentistry and her commitment to every patient is still as powerful today as it was when she first held a toothbrush.

How about you? How do you feel today about that central dream that drives you?

If we expect excellence, we tend find it. But, like all things in life, it has a way of being attracted to people who are committed to it.

Keeping it Real

"I've learned that people will forget what you said,
people will forget what you did, but people will never forget
how you made them feel." – Maya Angelou

One of my proudest small contributions during my three year Comcast adventure was my relationship with Frank Eliason. Frank and I were kindred spirits from the start, passionate about improving the customer experience and laser focused on finding root causes, broken processes, and areas for improvement. We often talked late into the night on our Instant Messengers about how to take our care efforts to the next level.

And that's how our Twitter initiative began.

I had been an early Twitter adopter, and when Summize developed a search function, it was only a nano-second before I started following the tweets about our company. Being a geek a heart and a believer in servant-leadership, I started proactively helping customers in my Division, regardless of whether or not they were in my Area of responsibility.

The focus was on being as transparent and as authentic as possible. Communicate clearly, be yourself, apologize for errors and work hard to fix it.

The results followed a unique and ultimately predictable pattern. What would start as a 140 character vitriolic blow torch could quickly turn a company hater into a fanatic fan.

And it was energizing to be solving problems and changing attitudes.

It was during one post-midnight IM session that I told Frank, "You oughta be doing this at headquarters. Just think of what you could learn. And how we could change the world!"

Frank is one of the smartest customer care guys I know and he did just that. The @comcastcares team he built literally transformed the company's image in a palpable, measurable way, he raised the customer service bar big time, and he became a social media icon in the process.

It's hard for large companies to be authentic and transparent. Size and scale are, by their very nature impersonal. You seek to distill the success formula to its essence and replicate it as fast and as profitably as possible. As you become more successful, the risk of failure is greater and the natural tendency is to hunker down and let someone else carefully do the talking for you.

Traditional public relations methodology is all about message management and reactive damage control. But in the Internet age, a new paradigm is emerging. The carefully crafted circular PR speak we all get from politicians, chief executives and their handlers, doesn't work in the lightning fast, viral pace of the social media culture.

We want straight talk from real people. We want them to talk with us, not to us. We want them to listen. And we expect them to respond... fast. We are starting to demand that they "relate" to us.

In the end, our ability to build a strong and personal relationship with our customers and business partners is the ONLY competitive advantage.

Just watch what goes on at Whole Foods, Disney World or Southwest Airlines and you'll see that people will accept other inconveniences and sometimes will pay higher prices to enjoy a better customer experience.

What distinguishes these guys from the rest of the pack?

You get the sense that these are real people who genuinely care about you. They use your name often. The ask questions and listen. Sometimes they guide you to another store, knowing that by getting you what you want somewhere else, you're likely to come back. They have personality.

Some of the best have the courage to be vulnerable. Frank certainly is. We all know and love his family, especially the angel he and Carolyn lost, but still love.

Frank will also, gently but firmly, call you out if your perceptions of the company are incorrect. Some real emotion is okay if it is authentic and focused on moving things forward.

Earlier this fall, I had the singular experience of spending an hour and a half with the President of Michigan State University. Dr. Lou Anna K. Simon is running a major academic institution in a state with a significantly troubled economy. The funding model for higher education is evolving right before our eyes and universities are having to re-invent themselves on the fly.

Lou Anna is everything Jim Collins' Good to Great Level 5 Leader should be. She is candid, she is transparent—answering our straight questions with equally straight answers—she is genuine in expressing the joys and frustrations that face her every day. And she lives the famous Stockdale Paradox, directly confronting the unpleasant current realities, without losing faith that the institution will ultimately prevail.

She won't remember this, but I asked her during Homecoming Weekend how she kept her attitude. "It's something you choose to do," she said. "I don't like the alternative."

Those are powerful words worth remembering.

As you enter your week, there's a lot to get done, a lot to worry about, and a lot of people depending on you to contribute to the forward movement of your organization.

Choose your attitude.
- Talk straight.
- Be transparent.
- Listen and respond.
- Have the courage to be who you really are.
- Appreciate others for who they really are.
- Never lose faith that "keeping it real" will ultimately get you to where you want to be.

How Winners Behave...in Defeat

"Courage consists of the power of self-recovery."
— *Ralph Waldo Emerson*

The best speech of the 2010 Final Four happened after Michigan State University lost to Butler in the semi-finals. MSU's Draymond Green gave it.

"We know we have to change a lot of things that we do as a team and as individuals. We have to go back and take a look in the mirror, realize who we are, how to do the things right that you need to do to win a championship."

There was no complaining about the officiating, which could have been better. In fact, Draymond's bear hug in the final seconds, probably saved coach Tom Izzo from a technical. There was no finger pointing. Just ownership and personal accountability.

Draymond Green demonstrated exactly how winners behave in that temporary space where the scoreboard doesn't reflect the ultimate outcome.

I was across town at a sports bar hosting 200 Spartan alumni at a game-watch party. Even though the second floor was primarily ours, about 100 Butler fans were cheering, just outside of the ropes that separated us.

It was frustrating to several of our guests. Alcohol fuels that frustration and there were some tense moments where we thought that it might boil over.

I learned long ago that magnanimity is the great defuser, so I worked every Butler fan in the crowd, shaking their hands and congratulating them on a well earned victory.

"Take that energy to the finals," I said. "Win it all and you'll make both of us proud."

Kindness, humility and an insatiable desire to learn from mistakes. These traits typify winners.

"Magnanimous people have no vanity," wrote Van Wyck Brooks. "They have no jealousy, and they feed on the true and the solid wherever they find it. And, what is more, they find it everywhere."

That's not easy to do when you have so much emotion invested in your team, or yourself.

William Temple believes that, "Humility does not mean thinking less of yourself than of other people, nor does it mean having a low opinion of your own gifts. It means freedom from thinking about yourself at all."

I recently gave some pretty direct feedback to some colleagues. One of them wrote me to say that she was hurt by it and took it personally.

Feedback is simply that. I told her to step outside of herself and look at the situation as a neutral third party. Digest what was useful and throw away the rest.

Often, some of our biggest detractors couldn't make a three point shot, close a deal or sustain a long term relationship. As Richard Rybolt says, "There will be a time when loud-mouthed, incompetent people seem to be getting the best of you. When that happens, you only have to be patient and wait for them to self destruct. It never fails."

Whatever you do, whether it's playing basketball, selling something, leading others or just interacting with your world, there will be times when people will exploit your perceived weaknesses and challenge your results. You will have setbacks and downright lousy days.

How you react will define you.

Turn the Prism

"A woman has many faces as she goes through her life. It's like we need more than one hair-do. We have many, many changes in the evolution of our lives. We have, we learn, and we grow; we view life differently, and life views us differently." — *Sharon Stone*

Remember when "reinventing the wheel" was a bad thing?

We currently live smack dab in the middle of an era that requires reinvention. Those tried and true patterns that used to guide us don't necessarily work anymore and the new stars will be those creative people who can look at the immense challenges we face and find a new way to meet them.

We all look at the world through a prism of paradigms. Our experience, education and corporate cultures are the tripod on which this prism is mounted. The sunlight that shines through it, paints colors on the synapses of our brains that generate the ideas we put into action.

What happens if you turn the prism?

One of the "4 Guidelines for 2009" I shared with our team during our annual retreat was to look at old problems in a new way, Turning the Prism of our paradigms to find out what fresh rainbows might be revealed. We then performed an anything-goes exercise. If we could waive a magic wand and make anything possible, what would we do?

You would be surprised at what magic can happen in this environment.

Example: When I was chairman of the Dreams Come True board in Jacksonville, Florida, our little office had traditionally lived, rent-free, on the largess of a kind board members who had extra space at their firms. We needed a our own building.

Paradigm: The tried and true game plan was to raise enough money from donors to build it. We determined that we would need 2.8 million dollars to get it done and began to identify people with big enough checkbooks to help us.

Turning the Prism: Along came a generous general contractor who believed in the cause. He said, "Let me see how much I can get donated." That turned our prism. We approached a large and very famous land-owner in Jacksonville with the idea. He gave us 2 acres of prime business land. The contractor was able to get 100% of both the materials and labor donated by his suppliers and subs. I personally wired the place for video and Internet with volunteers from my company. Everyone had a blast and it felt great to put our own sweat equity towards such an important project. We continued to raise the 2.8 million anyway and it became an endowment to fund our brand new, mortgage-free, building's operation forever.

The further you can push this idea generator into your organization, the better. In our shop, we try to let the supervisor team do the reinventing. They are one step away from the customer and work everyday with our smartest team members: the front line employees.

Some key ideas to help you get started:

- Begin with the end in mind: Steven Covey's chestnut is still as valuable today as it was when he gave it to us in his Seven Habits of Highly Effective People. What is the end state? How does success look? How will you measure it?

- Start from the premise that all things are possible: It's easy to get mired in reasons why an idea won't work. Don't fall into that trap.
- Involve the stakeholders: The best ideas come from those who execute and benefit.
- Encourage Crazy: From the craziest ideas often come the best solutions. Pizza guys delivering cable boxes? Somebody suggested that to me and our "Pizza and a Movie" promotion came to be.
- Test on a small scale and celebrate failure: I like to encourage risk taking. We celebrate failure like Thomas Edison did: "I am not discouraged," he is quoted as saying, "because every wrong attempt discarded is another step forward." Several parallel tests can yield tweaks and learnings that can be leveraged. Sometimes it's a mix of processes that end up being the right idea. And eliminating the fear of failure is the most empowering thing you can do for a person.
- Be patient and be tenacious: If this stuff were easy, everybody would be doing it. The guy who invented the wildly popular Red Box DVD rental vending machines tried it years ago with video tapes and failed. He lives Winston Churchill's mantra, "Never give in. Never give in. Never, Never, Never." His company is forcing the formerly dominant video stores to turn their prisms big time.
- Foster a "Culture of Innovation": That's my marketing term for getting people to accept and even become excited about change. After all, we are in an environment where things MUST change if we are to survive.

Turning the prism can work well in the human resource realm, too.

One of my proudest moments was preserving a long term, loyal and dedicated player who was on the wrong seat on our bus. We turned the prism to discover what activities brought him the most joy, and found a way he could express that joy and continue to serve. I got push-back from the higher ups at first, but never lost faith in him. He has become a high performer and is highly respected in his new role. And most importantly, he's happy and is supercharged to come to work each day. Something that shows in his relationships and work product. Best of all, We continue to benefit from his wisdom, institutional memory and experience.

And what about you? What could happen if you turn the prism and look at your career, your relationships, and your behaviors through a different light?

On my fridge, my wife has a magnet that says "What would you do if you knew you could not fail?"

What would you do?

Turn the prism and that dream could become a reality.

The Wisdom of Jim Rohn

"Happiness is not something you postpone for the future; it is something you design for the present." – Jim Rohn

Back in the late 70s, I briefly flirted with a career in real estate. It wasn't my passion, so I didn't last long, but it put me at the center of the golden age of motivational speaking.

Sales people are driven by the affirmation that comes from closing the next big deal. So those of us in the trade were constantly on the lookout for people who could charge us up and sharpen our positive attitudes for a day that was often filled with hurdles and rejection.

This was the arena where Earl Nightingale, Denis Waitley, Tom Hopkins, Zig Ziglar and Jim Rohn worked their magic. These educators/philosophers were masters at distilling the essence of motivation into parables, short stories and sentences. I drilled hundreds of these into my brain over the years, to the point where they reflexively pop out as not-so-subtle reminders to help keep me on course.

Tom Hopkins — *"I must do the most productive thing possible at every given moment."*

Zig Ziglar — *"Are you a wandering generality or a meaningful specific?"*

Earl Nightingale — *"We become what we think about."*

Denis Waitley — *"If you don't believe in something, you'll fall for anything."*

51

I post at least one of these short sound bytes on my @MSUScottW twitter feed each day. It's more of a reminder to myself to continue to practice the behaviors and attitudes that attract positive opportunities to serve, and like minded fellow travelers.

When Jim Rohn passed away in 2010, it was an opportunity to revisit the extraordinary life of this business philosopher.

He was born to an Idaho farming family on September 17, 1930. By his own account, at age 25 he was in a personal rut familiar to many middle-class families who were in debt, unable to see a way that would lead to his personal ambitions.

Around this time, he was introduced to John Earl Shoaff, an entrepreneur who impressed Jim with his wealth, business accomplishments, charisma and life philosophy. Jim joined Shoaff's direct sales organization, and began a process of personal development that culminated in his becoming a millionaire by age 31.

In the years that followed, Jim Rohn discovered a demand from people outside his industry to hear his rags to riches stories, and the personal development philosophy that he felt had led to his accomplishments.

Jim presented his seminars for more than 40 years. Wikipedia notes that he addressed over 6,000 audiences and 4 million people worldwide and authored 17 different books, audio and video programs.

Jim did not claim to teach novel truths, only fundamentals. As he was fond of saying: "There are no new fundamentals. Truth is not new, it is old. Whoever renders service to many puts himself in line for greatness – great wealth, great return, great satisfaction, great reputation, and great joy."

Jim saw five major puzzle pieces to life:

- **Philosophy:** how you think
- **Attitude:** how you feel
- **Action:** what you do
- **Results:** measure often to see if you are making progress
- **Lifestyle:** the kind of life you can make for yourself out of the first four pieces

How we dissect and develop each of these puzzle pieces will determine the joy or suffering we experience along the way.

One of my favorite hunting grounds is Twitter.com's search function: search.twitter.com. You can enter a word or phrase there and instantly get a feel for what the Twittersphere is thinking about it in the current moment. I regularly put "#quote" into the search box and let the wisdom of the ages wash over me in 140 characters or less.

Search Twitter for references to Jim Rohn and you will find a river of ideas. Ideas that are Jim's legacy. Ideas that can still inspire all of us to be our best.

Whether you write them on post-it notes and stick them on your bathroom mirror, post them on your desktop, or pass them on to friends, incorporating Jim Rhon's wisdom into your daily drill can help guide you to higher productivity, more joyful relationships and the kind of happiness that is the true definition of success.

Here are a few examples:

- Take care of your body. It's the only place you have to live.

- You cannot change your destination overnight, but you can change your direction overnight.
- You don't get paid for the hour. You get paid for the value you bring to the hour.
- We get paid for bringing value to the market place.
- Time is more valuable than money. You can get more money, but you can't get more time.
- Formal education will make you a living self-education will make you a fortune.
- Success is doing ordinary things extraordinarily well.
- Your philosophy determines whether you will go for the disciplines or continue the errors.
- Work harder on yourself than you do on your job.
- Without a sense of urgency, desire loses its value.
- Whatever good things we build end up building us.
- We must all suffer one of two things: the pain of discipline or the pain of regret or disappointment.
- The more you know the less you need to say.
- Don't wish it was easier—wish you were better.
- The few who do, are the envy of the many who only watch.
- Success is nothing more than a few simple disciplines, practiced every day.
- Its not the blowing of the wind, but the set of the sail that determines your outcome.
- Success is not to be pursued; it is to be attracted by the person you become.
- The book you don't read won't help.
- If you are not willing to risk the unusual, you will have to settle for the ordinary.
- Give whatever you are doing and whoever you are with the gift of your attention.
- Either you run the day or the day runs you.

- Discipline is the bridge between goals and accomplishment.
- The major value in life is not what you get. The major value in life is what you become.

For more about this fascinating man, visit jimrohn.com

The Night Tom Izzo
Became a Spartan for Life

"Ladies and gentleman, It is my privilege, and my honor to tell you tonight that Tom Izzo will be staying in the MSU Family!*"*
- Spoken to 600 people at the MSUAA Berrien County Steak & Suds Event

Every June, the Berrien Springs Spartans throw the largest MSU Alumni steak cook out in the world. 650 people come from Michigan, Indiana and Illinois to enjoy grilled ribeye, salad and strawberry dessert. Colleen and I were serving steaks when I got the text from Mark Hollis.

There would be a press conference at 8:30PM.

It had been a stressful ten days for my Spartan partner and friend. As Athletic Director for one of the most successful programs in the NCAA, Mark knows that it's all about leadership.

And we had the best in Tom Izzo. Our basketball coach had grown from assistant to legend in nearly two decades at MSU. He runs a stellar program that focuses as much on academics and life after sports as it does on Final Four appearances.

Dan Gilbert knew all of this. And as the primary owner of the Cleveland Cavaliers NBA franchise, he had been putting a full court press on Coach Izzo to come and join his team.

As the days passed, the tension increased. Would Tom leave our Beloved Institution?

I popped "Izzo" into my iPhone's twitter search engine and could see that more and more media outlets were sharing what I already knew. ESPN had the University's official statement. Magnanimous and class personified. From President Simon to Athletic Director Hollis to The Coach himself, it was a message for the history books, distilled to just eight words.

Tom Izzo would be a Spartan for LIfe.

When we finished serving the crowd and all the prize drawings had concluded, Dave Brown, the most familiar face at the MSU Alumni Association, took the microphone and gave me a kind introduction.

There were many things I was thinking:

Our great Institution is the Beacon that will help Michigan reinvent herself—leaner, greener, smarter—a phoenix rising from industrial ash to soar to new heights.

Michigan State University will educate and inspire many more graduates to build careers right here in the Great Lakes State.

Our 800 student athletes will inevitably join all Spartan alumni to become the intellectual fuel that fires the American Dream.

Exceptional role models like our faculty and staff have exactly the same powerful influence on young lives that more familiar names like Izzo, Dantonio, Comley and Merchant have in the rarified climes of Division I athletics.

President Simon has created a culture where the most well known Spartan names are as humble and as dedicated to the MSU ethic as are the greenest graduate assistants.

All these elements mixed in my heart as I told the crowd, "It is my privilege, and my honor to tell you tonight that Tom Izzo will be staying in the MSU Family."

The reaction of the crowd is something I can't describe in words, except to say that the ovation was so stunning that I thought I could see the tops of the huge tents rise in response.

Dave Brown has seen many memorable Spartan moments in his 20 plus years at MSUAA. He would later relate that this was one of his favorites. He whispered, "You just became the most popular guy here."

But I was just a humble messenger, scratching the surface of the vast aquifer that is the worldwide impact of Michigan State University.

Colleen and I stole away to our car and made our way, as fast as we could, back to East Lansing. Along the way, we listened to Tom's press conference. There were cautionary tales about how inaccuracies and untruths can easily spread in the Internet age. We got a first hand feel for what it's like to live under the public microscope, and how The Coach and his family handled it with courage and grace, even as others did not.

And we heard Tom talk about his love for The State of Michigan; for his family; and for the many people, players, fellow coaches and friends who helped him see farther and climb higher. In the process of that climb, he took all of us with him. Teaching us about discipline, about leadership and about the complicated and challenging process of turning boys into men.

As the press conference ended, we were coming up on the Trowbridge overpass. "We have to stop by and give our support to Lou Anna, Mark and Tom," Colleen said.

So, dressed in our jeans and grease spotted steak server outfits, we turned toward campus.

The satellite trucks still lined the curbs in front of the Clara Bell Smith Center. But we were naturally drawn to the Brez, the bricks and mortar symbol of the Spartan Basketball legacy. We got out of the car and drank in the evening, making a memory. It was a humid night. The radar said that storms were headed our way. And the IM fields were still alight as youngsters who play what the rest of the world calls "football," kicked soccer balls back and forth on the Spartan green grass.

Colleen and I walked toward the basketball offices and saw a familiar face. Lupe Izzo, the quintessential sports mom, was texting Raquel and probably thinking about the next morning, when Steven's summer activities would require her to be coach, chef, chauffeur and psychologist.

We could relate. Colleen did the bulk of the heavy lifting when Shelby and Brandon were that age.

We told her how happy we were that the ordeal was over, asked after her mother, and wondered if she was happy with the outcome. Her smile said it all.

Then The Coach emerged; sport coat, open collar, looking more relaxed than anybody who had survived the past week's onslaughts had a right to be. He greeted us warmly like the family we all are.

I struggled with my emotions.

In 30 years as a business executive, I've come to understand the spotlight. How hard it can be for children to have a normal life in the shadow of a parent who is closely identified with a controversial brand. How our soul mates often become an extension of the good or bad that may happen in our professional world and how the ones we love most are forced to spend too many hours without us there.

This is the flip side of the notoriety that comes with achievement.

The Izzos are magnificent role models in a universe where too few can survive uncommon success. To know that these extraordinary people would continue to inspire and teach us made both Colleen and me realize how lucky we are to be living and working in the same educational community with Tom and Lupe.

And at that moment, I felt the energy of all 500,000 Michigan State University alumni surging a single word through my body.

Gratitude.

Opening Night

The night began at Munn. MSU / OSU at 6:30. There's an aroma at an ice palace that is incomparable. It's a mixture of frozen water, popcorn, sharpened steel and sweat. It's sweet and sour, cold and hot. And there's nothing like feeling the power of a check against the boards when a Spartan defenseman nails a winger. This, win or lose, is the uninhibited joy that die-hard MSU Hockey fans know.

I grew up on this stuff in Ann Arbor, where we all played the game, and more than a few of us have some false teeth to prove it. When I came to MSU I was a regular, starting back in the days when the venue was Demonstration Hall, and students could lace our skates and ply the same ice on the weekends when the Spartans didn't play.

Tonight we were in command of the ice. It felt a little strange to leave before it was over, especially with an uncharacteristic 60 degree November evening on the outside. But I had another engagement.

The fall of 2010 was officially my second Basketball Season as the MSU Alumni Guy, and I wanted to be there to drink in every minute. I've been around long enough to recognize a hundred faces along the way. We're not lulled into complacency by a string of Final Four appearances. We Spartans have been burned too many times on two many fields to take anything for granted. But this year there is a particular excitement surrounding the Jack Breslin Events Center. We call it "The Brez".

Coach Izzo is a Spartan for life. He has a strong front five and an impressive bench. And he has the Izzone. Oft imitated but never equalled. The most potent, most feared student section in the NCAA. And tonight the kids on the court and the kids in the stands start the 2010-2011 season.

It's just minutes before the 8:30 tip-off. I enter through Will-Call. My All-Area pass lets me walk down the two flights to the ground floor and right past the door of the locker room. The Big Ten Network camera is already poised outside. It's moments before the gladiators will emerge.

I turn right, into the tunnel and see Kevin Pauga, KP to everybody who knows him. He's the unheralded extension of The Coach, the guy who attends to a thousand details, who is the first to hear the heat when something goes wrong and the first to jump into the fray to make it right. Even though he knows this drill by heart, his eyes dart in a hundred directions, looking for any inconsistency, ready to make whatever adjustments so that the machine that is Spartan Basketball will run with well oiled efficiency.

We shake hands. In spite of the thousand things on his mind, he is happy to see me and we exchange a few supportive words.

I enter the arena and stand just to the right of the tunnel. This is my favorite spot. In front of me sit the favored press, a dozen working journalists who will watch the game from the front lines, feel the sweat and the heat that radiates off of ten young men who will focus on one thing tonight: winning. I know most of them by now, so the recognition is mutual, although our roles are on opposite poles of the magnet. They are here to analyze, critique and document every nuance of the game. I'm here to throw more gas on the energetic fire in the stands.

The music swells, the Izzone thunders it's approval and the Spartans emerge. Those who have worn the these jerseys will tell you that this moment is addicting. It's the adrenaline rush that reassures and sharpens their focus to a laser point.

For any opponent unfortunate enough to have to play in this maelstrom, it's downright intimidating.

By now I'm working my way through the izzone. It will take me 20 minutes to hit every row, because the troops nearly encircle the lower bowl. I waive to Chris, Wonder, Megan several score of the members I have come to know well. Despite my green jacket, white shirt, and the identifying MSUAA name tag, the majority of the Izzone is oblivious to my presence.

They are already into their traditional moves, poking at the opposition, supercharging the home team and turning the Brez into a cacophony of distraction whenever the other side has the ball. This year, the Izzone has moved to the East side of the arena. It's a better shot for the TV cameras and it puts the loudest lungs right behind the visitors bench. The enemy is deafened whenever they get the ball so the communication on the floor is non verbal and often ineffectual.

By contrast, when the Spartans are in control there is dead silence punctuated by explosive support whenever there is an MSU basket. Before the mid-point of the first half, I've gone up and down every stairway in the lower bowl. I'm drenched to the skin with sweat and loving every minute of it.

Tonight the alumni band is there. Nearly all of The Spartan Brass double in the marching band and they are competing in another venue, so a grayer crowd plays the fight song this November evening. I know most of these guys and am beyond impressed when I listen from across the arena. I can hear every part, executed clearly, perfectly and at a volume that would make John Madden proud.

Now it's time to work the boxes and platforms that ring the mid-level of the arena. I stop in at every one and greet the rarified revelers who, by investment, or by luck, have some of the best seats in the house. Since it's the first game of the season and the Big Ten contests are still weeks away, many of the rollers have shared their abundance with their team members. These are the people who do the real work and rarely get to fully enjoy the game experience. They are having the time of their lives as we ply them with food, drink and appreciation.

The trustee boxes are more subdued. Here are the elected fiduciaries who carry the burden of sustaining the Institution through thick and thin. And these days in Michigan, everything is thinner.

They know, just as Coach Izzo does, that it's a long way to Houston. We'll win some and lose some. But this first game will give the practiced eyes a good feel for the mettle and commitment the warriors will need to go the distance. I share a common history with most of these people, so we talk about old battles fought in our corporate incarnations even as we watch the moves of Lucius, Lucas and Green with microscopic eyes. Eyes that notice the improvements that are the product of off season dedication, hours in the weight room, and even more hours dedicated to that heavy burden of academic and athletic performance that is the higher standard to which all student-athletes are held.

Tonight the team looks confident. As the lead grows, they sometimes slow down. Too many foul shots are missed. Izzo won't tolerate that and we imagine the intensity of the feedback that awaits in the locker room, and the personalized assignments each player will be given to sharpen their edge between tonight and the next game.

Tomorrow, I know that Suzi Merchant will ply these same waters. The crowds are thinner for the women, but those who are there are no less dedicated and probably even more vocal. And to focus on excellence is equal to the higher profile sports that always get more column inches of analysis.

The Coach and the players of both basketball genders share the same two athletic goals: Make it to the Final Four, and showcase talent that may someday be worthy of the professional ranks. But behind the curtain, there is the Institution in all it's academic glory. The University that will do its best to prepare these kids for what most likely will morph from plan "B" to plan "A": a profession beyond the basketball court.

I'm lucky to know a few of the inner workings. We don't pay lip service to the lessons off the court. Players are held accountable for performance in the classroom, even as weeknight away games rack up absences that some professors won't excuse. And we try to teach them about the character of adulthood. It's a rough curriculum for some, who may have only known the law of the street, and not everybody will learn it. But it's the ultimate lesson that Izzo, Merchant, Comley,

Dantonio and 21 other varsity coaches constantly teach every day.

I climb into the upper bowl, to the last row at the upper reaches of the Nosebleed section. From the highest promontory, I survey the confluence of athleticism, fan support and the extraordinary ambiance of a venue that is loved by the faithful and feared by everyone else.

This is Spartan Basketball. It is the house that Judd built and Izzo has perpetuated into a dynasty. A program that is the envy of a thousand other coaches. And an experience that inspires and satisfies, even on the rare occasions when the outcome is in the opponents' favor.

I look at the championship banners that ring the rafters and remember those who have come before, building the foundations on which this marvelous facility now stands.

And give thanks, once again, that I am a Spartan.

The Stockdale Paradox

"You must never confuse faith that you will prevail in the end – which you can never afford to lose – with the discipline to confront the most brutal facts of your current reality, whatever they might be." – Jim Stockdale

---

Whenever I get the chance to lead a new team, the first book I share with them is Jim Collins' *Good to Great*. In it, Jim and his gifted group of inquisitive smart people dissect the commonalities that make for uncommonly great long term performance.

If you don't yet own this book, go out and buy it immediately. If you do own it, turn with me now to the section where Jim outlines "The Stockdale Paradox".

Back in the mid '80s, I was working as the marketing guy for Continental Cablevision on Washington Square in downtown Lansing, Michigan. Part of my daily ritual was listening to Dick Estell's Radio Reader program on WKAR.

One winter, I was riveted by Dick's reading of Admiral Jim Stockdale's story of the seven years he spent as the highest ranking prisoner of war at the Hanoi Hilton. Titled *In Love and War*, with alternating chapters written by his wife Sybil, Stockdale took me through his excruciating experience of physical and emotional torture at the hand of the North Vietnamese. And how he inspired the POWs to continue to fight from within the walls of their prison.

In Love and War is still in my personal library, well worn from many readings, so when Jim Collins introduced his readers to "The Stockdale Paradox" in *Good to Great*, I paid particular attention.

In a nutshell, "The Stockdale Paradox" is this:

Face the unpleasant realities but don't lose faith in the ultimate outcome.

If there was ever a touchstone for the challenges our world faces today, this is it.

Here is the current reality: Whatever you do for a living, it is likely that the economic foundations that underpin your gig are tenuous. Layoffs and cutbacks abound. We are being asked to do more with less. There is not enough budget money to get the job done the way we have done it before. The debate about strategies and tactics to get us where we want to be does not reveal a clear pathway.

Jim Stockdale's advice? Deal with it.

Stop complaining, start thinking and act.

As Jim Stockdale realized, prevailing is not something that happens in the script of a two hour movie. It is an iterative process, full of steps forward and backward, dead ends and rabbit holes. It is the day-to-day energy you must invest to survive and thrive, no matter what. In the end, Stockdale did prevail and he felt that his seven years as a POW were the defining years of his life, "something, in retrospect, I would not change."

Viktor Frankl discovered something similar while immersed in the horror of the Holocaust during the Second World War. In his seminal work *Man's Search For Meaning* he says, "Most men in a concentration camp believed that the real opportunities of life had passed. Yet, in reality, there was an opportunity and a challenge. One could make a victory of those experiences, turning life into an inner triumph, or one could ignore the challenge and simply vegetate, as did a majority of the prisoners."

How many vegitators do you know?

Something that both Frankl and Stockdale shared was faith that their daily contributions would ultimately lead to a productive objective. Perhaps not the same faith we speak of on Sundays but something very similar. As C. S. Lewis puts it, "Faith is merely the virtue by which we hold to our reasoned ideas, despite moods to the contrary."

So what does all of this stuff mean to you? And how can you use The Stockdale Paradox to your advantage.

Whatever your current situation — Deal with it!

- What data do you need to analyze where you are now with the cold, unbiased eye of a consultant?
- If you left your body and looked at your world as a witness, what opportunities do you see?
- How can you engage to maximize them?
- Who can you collaborate with to find win-win scenarios for both sides?
- How do you assess your fitness to survive and thrive in this uncomfortable current reality?
- What strengths do you bring?
- What skills do you need to develop?

- Who can be your teachers?
- Who can travel with you and add value along the way?
- What can you contribute, beyond your work relationships, to help those community causes you care about?
- What are those things beyond career and family that epitomize for you Churchill's maxim, "We make a living with what we get but make a life by what we give"?

Ponder the questions carefully. Write them down and answer them honestly. They will give you a clear and realistic, if painful, picture of your current reality and will help you begin to develop game plans to grow.

Think about the big picture where you work. How can your contributions help the larger team not only survive but thrive? Believe it or not, the women and men in charge are feeling the same discomfort in the pits of their stomachs and will value any helpful input from any source that might make a difference.

You could make that difference.

Do not give up. History is littered with stories of how "the race is not always to the swift, nor the strong, but to those who persevere."

As Emerson wrote, "Our greatest glory is not in never failing, but in rising up every time we fail."

So get up and start the race anew.

Keep Jim Stockdale in mind as you face your challenges. Be aware of the power of perseverance. As Bill Feather says, "Success seems to be largely a matter of hanging on after others let go."

Deal with your current reality. Keep the faith that you will prevail and you will.

Hang in there!

Alan

"The difference between a stumbling block and a stepping stone is how you decide use them."

One Spring day during my cable TV career, I traveled to Atlanta to attend the National Cable Telecommunications Association convention. Most travelers take the taxi from the airport to downtown, but since I was traveling on the largesse of the Company, a buck seventy-five MARTA ride felt more responsible than a twenty dollar cab fare.

So it was that I emerged from the caverns beneath Peachtree Plaza, squinting into the afternoon sun, searching among the canyons of steel and cement for my hotel.

"Where ya headed?"

He was five foot nothing and dressed in the somewhat ragged attire we used to discourage the kids from wearing in public. But he looked much older. Like the majority of my MARTA companions, his ancestors had likely been forcibly emigrated from Africa. He seemed to be without portfolio.

"Where ya headed," he repeated.

"Can you tell me the way to the Marriott Marquis?"

"I can do better than that, follow me."

His manner was friendly, almost as if he might even be a hotel employee.

"I'm Alan, and you are?"

"Scott."

"Where do you hail from, Scott?"

"Just in from Illinois," I said. I felt slightly uneasy sharing too much information with this stranger.

"Welcome to Atlanta, Scott. Where in Illinois, Chicago, Peoria?"

"Moline."

"Don't know it." Alan eyed my wheeled suitcase and the plastic covering that protected my hanging attire. "You look like you're here on business, Scott."

"Yep, a convention." I wanted to change the subject. "Tell me about yourself, Alan. What do you do in Atlanta?"

"During the week, I'm in the labor pool and on weekends I'm a homeless tour guide."

A homeless tour guide. I remembered talking with some homeless folks in Chicago. They wore orange safety vests, and seemed to earn money picking up trash in the city parks. But this guy sounded like an entrepreneur.

"I appreciate the company," I said. It was a stretch. I always like to find my own way, and like most middle class whites, my paradigms of the homeless made me uncomfortable getting too closely involved with someone who might have more interest in the content of my wallet than in the content of my character.

But Alan was undeterred.

"Your hotel is just around the corner. We'll head down Harris and turn left. If it's raining when you have to head back to the airport, there's actually a covered walkway that takes you right to Peachtree plaza. What kind of food do you like to eat, Scott?"

I recognized this as one of the qualifying questions we teach our sales folks to ask whenever they were with a customer. Learn about their likes and you can tailor the product benefits to meet their special needs. It increases your chance of making a sale.

"I'm easy," I said, "as long as it isn't Mexican or too spicy."

Alan launched into a detailed description of the key restaurants in the neighborhood, painting vivid word pictures of the ambiance, the specialty of the house and the price range.

By now we were at the hotel's valet entrance.

"Here's your hotel, Scott. Do you have any questions for me?"

It must be time for a tip. I opened my wallet and drew out a ten.

"I've really enjoyed our conversation," I said. "Do you accept gratuities for this service?"

Alan looked offended. It was a well practiced act.

"I'm not a panhandler. I'm just a homeless tour guide trying to get off the street."

Panhandling seemed to be a magic word. I had a vague memory of a news story about how Atlanta had recently enacted an ordinance banning the practice downtown. The ACLU was in the process of suing the City to stop its enforcement.

I pressed the Hamilton into Alan's palm. "Well I hope this helps. Thanks very much for taking such good care of me."

"How long you in town, Scott?"

"Here till Tuesday."

"I'll see you around."

Alan sauntered off into the lengthening shadows. I watched him go and pondered the economic gulf that separated us, and the humanity we had shared for ten minutes that spring day. The law said he couldn't simply ask for money anymore. But Alan had figured out a way around the obstacle, proof that even at the most fundamental levels of existence, necessity is still the mother of invention.

It's About Time

Do you ever notice how the most successful people always seem to be willing to share their time? But, spend some of that time with them and you will quickly see that they want to invest it carefully. If they sense you are not benefiting, they will either quickly correct your behavior or disconnect and move on.

Whatever your passion, time is the one commodity that most important. How you use it will determine the amount of happiness or suffering you will encounter along the way.

Alan Lakein wrote the time management classic *How to Get Control of Your Time and Your Life*. He implores us to establish SMART (specific, measurable, achievable, related/relevant, and time framed) goals. And here is the key: Prioritize them using an A to C system. "A" goals are at the top of the list, are most important and should get 80% of your time. At the other end of the spectrum are "C" goals. Unfortunately, most people spend 80% of their time "majoring in minors". Watching TV, video games, even things like cutting the grass and shopping can fall into this category.

Dartmouth College distributes these time management tips to new freshman, based on Lakein's book:
- Count all your time as time to be used and make every attempt to get satisfaction out of every moment.

76

- Find something to enjoy in whatever you do.
- Try to be an optimist and seek out the good in your life.
- Find ways to build on your successes.
- Stop regretting your failures and start learning from your mistakes.
- Remind yourself, "There is always enough time for the important things." If it is important, you should be able to make time to do it.
- Continually look at ways of freeing up your time.
- Examine your old habits and search for ways to change or eliminate them.
- Try to use waiting time; review notes or do practice problems.
- Keep paper or a calendar with you to jot down the things you have to do or notes to yourself.
- Examine and revise your lifetime goals on a monthly basis and be sure to include progress towards those goals on a daily basis.
- Put up reminders in your home or office about your goals.
- Always keep those long term goals in mind.
- Plan your day each morning or the night before and set priorities for yourself.
- Maintain and develop a list of specific things to be done each day, set your priorities and the get the most important ones done as soon in the day as you can. Evaluate your progress at the end of the day briefly.
- Look ahead in your month and try and anticipate what is going to happen so you can better schedule your time.
- Try rewarding yourself when you get things done as you had planned, especially the important ones.
- Do first things first.
- Have confidence in yourself and in your judgement of priorities and stick to them no matter what.

- When you catch yourself procrastinating, ask yourself, "What am I avoiding?"
- Start with the most difficult parts of projects, then either the worst is done or you may find you don't have to do all the other small tasks.
- Catch yourself when you are involved in unproductive projects and stop as soon as you can.
- Find time to concentrate on high priority items or activities.
- Concentrate on one thing at a time.
- Put your efforts in areas that provide long term benefits.
- Push yourself and be persistent, especially when you know you are doing well.
- Think on paper when possible. It makes it easier to review and revise.
- Be sure and set deadlines for yourself whenever possible.
- Delegate responsibilities whenever possible.
- Ask for advice when needed.

When I was a kid, my dad and I had many conversations about "balance". For me, balance was about cramming as much fun, and as little work into every day. Dad taught me that it was important to properly balance your time investments toward the care of your mind, body and spirit.

Some days this meant focusing much of my time on filling my brain with the knowledge that could help me make more effective decisions. During the course of the week, he modeled the behavior by investing regular time in his personal fitness plan (he still does it today, at age 85). And both of my parents taught me the value of investing time to nurture the right relationships.

It took me awhile to figure out what those "right relationships" were, but I came around to an understanding that it's best to build friendships with people who radiate positive energy.

We all know energy suckers, those unfortunates who always talk about themselves, wear their travails like war wounds, and love to talk about how the world is going to hell in a hand basket. They thrive on sucking the energy out of you and the end of each encounter leaves you emotionally exhausted.

So pick your friends like you would a growth-stock. If the fundamentals look good, take a chance and invest. But make sure you're getting a return on the investment.

Since our time is truly the universal coin of the realm, plan how you will spend it. Carefully and candidly assess what you have spent and re-allocate your time each day to what yields the best intellectual, spiritual and physiological benefits.

One of the most interesting people I met during the past year worked for Human Resources at Comcast. It is her belief that we exist in heaven or hell, depending on two things: our attitude toward what happens to us, and how we spend our time responding to it.

Ponder that one as you attack the opportunities that face you. We can't always control what may happen to us, but we're truly the only ones who really control how we spend time responding to it.

If you're currently "between opportunities" (my definition of being jobless), how can you creatively and effectively invest your time to engage in the next phase of your career?

If you are unsure of what you want to be when you grow up (I still sometimes am), what things can you spend time on to help clarify the picture and point you towards action steps to focus on a dream.

Steve Jobs says, "Your time is limited, so don't waste it living someone else's life. Don't be trapped by dogma – which is living with the results of other people's thinking. Don't let the noise of other's opinions drown out your own inner voice. And most important, have the courage to follow your heart and intuition. They somehow already know what you truly want to become. Everything else is secondary."

If you're not where you want to be right now, consider honestly how you spend your time.

Modify your portfolio and you may well discover that you can generate a much more effective return on your investment.

What is Power

*"I hope our wisdom will grow with our power,
and teach us that the less we use our power
the greater it will be." – Thomas Jefferson*

I was the new guy in Jacksonville. Not yet in the seat, but about to become the vice president in charge of 640 people and a market of over a million. It was the day before I was to start. To get the lay of the land, I visited the local home and garden show.

Our company had a booth there and I watched, at first from afar, to see how well we were received by the attendees. Sandra and Jamie were our representatives, both gregarious, well trained and helpful.

I walked up and casually began asking questions. They were friendly and responsive. And then I said something that gave me away. I'm not sure what it was but Sandra looked me over and said, "You're the new VP."

I was busted, so I came clean. "Yup, I start tomorrow. You guys are doing a terrific job!"

It was then that I saw how others can perceive power. To Sandra, what I was had little bearing on who I was. She kept on talking, shifting gears to where she saw opportunity to improve our business processes and better serve our customers.

Jamie clammed up. I learned later that she told Sandra afterwards, "How could you talk like that to our new vice president?"

We all tend to be in awe of the powerful. When we know that someone has power, we listen more carefully and are circumspect in how we answer. We respond more quickly to their requests and try to curry their favor because we believe that they can influence our destiny.

In some organizational cultures, titles are everything. Rank has its privileges, the saying goes, and many of us spend our careers chasing it.

Over the years, my teams have grown weary of my telling the tale of the Servant Leader. Lao-Tzu defined the concept this way around 500 B.C.: "The highest type of ruler is one of whose existence the people are barely aware. Next comes one whom they love and praise. Next comes one whom they fear. Next comes one whom they despise and defy. When you are lacking in faith, others will be unfaithful to you. The Sage is self-effacing and scanty of words. When his task is accomplished and things have been completed, all the people say, 'We ourselves have achieved it.'"

In the gospels, Jesus is said to have told his followers, "You know that the rulers of the Gentiles lord it over them, and their high officials exercise authority over them. Not so with you. Instead, whoever wants to become great among you must be your servant, and whoever wants to be first must be your slave—just as the Son of Man did not come to be served, but to serve, and to give his life as a ransom for many."

Robert Greenleaf is a personal hero of mine. He was an AT&T executive who studied servant leadership extensively. In his pamphlet, "The Servant as Leader" he writes, "The servant-leader is servant first. It begins with the natural feeling that one wants to serve, to serve first. Then conscious choice brings one to aspire to lead. That person is sharply different from one who is leader first, perhaps because of the need to assuage an unusual power drive or to acquire material possessions. The leader-first and the servant-first are two extreme types. Between them there are shadings and blends that are part of the infinite variety of human nature."

"The difference manifests itself in the care taken by the servant-first to make sure that other people's highest priority needs are being served. The best test, and difficult to administer, is: Do those served grow as persons? Do they, while being served, become healthier, wiser, freer, more autonomous, more likely themselves to become servants? And, what is the effect on the least privileged in society? Will they benefit or at least not be further deprived?"

Larry Spears, longtime head of the Greenleaf Center for Servant Leadership, identified ten characteristic of servant leaders in Greenleaf's writings:

- listening
- empathy
- healing
- awareness
- persuasion
- conceptualization
- foresight
- stewardship
- commitment to the growth of others
- building community

No matter what your title may be, it is possible for you to exert your personal servant power to positively influence others. Help them solve their problems and they are more likely to help you solve yours.

I tell my team, "First seek to serve, find out where it hurts and help make it better."

The old sales maxim goes: You must first build rapport before you can earn the right to ask for the order. Too many of us come into the room with our sales pitch already underway.

During one of my weekly one-on-one meetings with my team, one of my colleagues asked, "How can I earn respect from someone who is hung up on hierarchy?"

We can earn just about anyone's regard by helping them build their own self respect. This doesn't mean capitulating on your principles, or knuckling under to a bully. It does mean choosing carefully how and when we react. As Stephen Covey says, "Between stimulus and response is our greatest power – the freedom to choose."

Seek to understand why the other person is responding they way they do. Ask clarifying questions. Practice Greenleaf's ten characteristics of servant leaders. Then watch the magic happen. If it does not, bring your boss into it. As your servant, she can help remove the obstacles to your growth and success.

My relationship mentor Keith Ferrazzi says that getting only happens when you give without expectation of return. That is hard to do when each of us has metrics to deliver to our organization and to our loved ones, but it is truly the only way that real returns will accrue.

When the time comes where you are given a title that bestows power upon your shoulders, remember that you are still a servant, you just have a bigger constituency who are depending on you.

Your greatest power is the power to serve others. Do it joyfully, patiently and tenaciously.

Dr. Martin Luther King, Jr. once said, "I am not interested in power for power's sake, but I'm interested in power that is moral, that is right and that is good".

As you express your personal power in this pivotal time in our nation's history, remember, too, John F. Kennedy's cautionary words.

"We have the power to make this the best generation of mankind in the history of the world – or to make it the last."

I choose the former.

What I Learned at Harvard Business School

"You give your best and good things happen." – *Salem*

In June of 2006, I went to Harvard. My company sent me to do some post graduate studies focusing on customer service and business metrics. It was a great week. Intense, exhausting and fun. But I realized early on that my real education began before the first class even began.

- Tangible Value
- Clear Strategy
- Committed Team
- Excellent Execution

Those are the four take-aways from my experience at Harvard Business School. The professors were excellent. I was surrounded by smart people who were engaged and eager to learn. The atmosphere was conducive to learning, the technology was top notch and the food was first rate.

But if I had been paying attention, I would have learned everything I needed to know the moment I got off the plane.

When I heard I was going to Cambridge, I have to admit that my heart sank. I would have to endure Logan Airport and the Daedalusian maze that Bostonians call ground transportation.

I've written before about my preference for trains. The travel tips the college provided ignore the T, Boston's rail transit system, and probably for good reason. Although it costs a fraction of a cab ride, it's a hike to get from the Harvard Square Station to the HBS facility, and the footbridge across the Charles River is not conducive to wheeled luggage.

That left the taxi cabs. I don't have a beef with Boston cabbies. They have a well deserved reputation for eclecticism in ethnic origin and personality. But the cab line at Logan's Terminal C will instantly generate strong commentary from the regulars who must endure it's winding queue.

It didn't help that my connection arrived at 6:40 and that the opening reception was scheduled for 7. When I travel, the company considers Sundays an adjunct to the five day work week. And since my family time is my most prized possession, I do my best to book the last boat out. Airtran delivered on it's promise this particular trip, and thanks to my strict carry-on luggage policy, I was at the end of the queue at 6:50 on the button.

The muttering of the regulars seemed to concur that from our remote position, we had an hour wait for a ride into town. That's when Salem appeared and my lesson in the four take-aways began.

"Where are you going?"

He seemed to be taking a transportation survey among those of us at the tail end of the cab line. Many simply ignored his question, but four of us mumbled answers.

"We can do that. Follow me."

A woman left her place in line and, with group dynamics in full sway, the rest of our quartet followed. We reentered the terminal and rode the escalator to the departure level.

87

"What's this all about," I asked the guy in front of me.

"You'll see."The guy knew something I didn't.

Beyond the sliding doors there stood a spotless mini-van, a transportation company name stenciled on the door panel. The rear gate was open and Salem began tossing our luggage in the back.

"The front door of your hotel, 20 dollars," he said to the first woman. He rattled off prices to the rest of us, finishing mine with a final flourish, "Harvard Business School, 30 dollars."

I scanned my memory of Harvard transpo memorandum. "cab rides from Logan airport typically cost between 40 and 50 dollars." Tangible value. This would be cheaper. We all climbed aboard.

"I always pick my own customers," Salem said as we sped away from Terminal C. "I find people who are going in the same general direction, charge less and take as many as I can."

The Thomas P. O'Neil Tunnel connects Logan with the rest of the world. We were headed in that direction now and I could quickly see a line of about 150 cars crawling three abreast toward the toll booths. Salem seemed to be ignoring them as he raced along in the far right lane.

"Do you have one of those toll transponders that let you bypass this mess," I wondered?

"I'm special," was Salem's grinning response. At that instant, we arrived at the front of the toll line and he cut the wheel to the left, sliding into a non-existent space between a vehicle and the toll booth. Salem waived his left hand in a friendly greeting that was met with a sonorous blast and a hail of epithets. We were now at the front of the line.

"I pick my own customers, charge less and give them excellent service," he said. Clear strategy.

We shot away from the toll booth and were soon threading our way among the traffic in the tunnel. The speed limit therein was 45 miles per, but my eyes saw the speedometer top 60.

"Nobody gets people to where they want to be more quickly than me. My cab is the cleanest and I never make my customers listen to these." He pointed to an array of CDs clipped to his visor. It was an interesting mix of heavy metal and Arabic. Salem seemed to read our thoughts.

"After 9-11, people are afraid of anyone who looks like an Arab," he said. "But I love the United States and I love Americans. "And this," he turned to look at us with his right arm outstretched, "is the realization of my dreams."

We were on the Sturrow Drive now, doing 80. Fenway park slid quickly by on the left. Salem's lesson continued. "My daughter was born here. She will go to college on scholarship, perhaps to medical school. I tell her, 'You give your best and good things happen'. This is how I work. To be the best. To show her that this is true." Commitment, clear and simple.

I watched as he dropped off each customer. All gave him more than quoted fee. He had earned 30% in tips by the time we pulled up the front of McKinley Hall. The entire experience had taken place in 20 minutes. By my calculation, I would be checked in and in the reception hall with time to spare.

Excellent execution.

I gave him fifty dollars.

I thought of Salem many times during the next five days. The Harvard experience was well worth the investment. But even now I smile as I think of how I learned the essence of sustainable success from a Boston cabbie.

How am I Doing?

"It is a capital mistake to theorize before one has data. Insensibly one begins to twist facts to suit theories, instead of theories to suit facts." – Sherlock Holmes from A Scandal in Bohemia

One of my favorite phrases comes from Ken Blanchard, author of *The One Minute Manager*: "Feedback is the breakfast of champions."

Todd Storz, one of the inventors of Top 40 radio in the early 60s, is famously credited with keeping track of what songs people were playing in restaurant juke boxes and using that data to populate his on air playlist.

Richard Fatherley, a former Storz employee quotes Todd as saying, "I became convinced that people demand their favorites over and over while in the Army during the Second World War. I remember vividly what used to happen in restaurants here in the States. The customers would throw their nickels into the juke box and come up repeatedly with the same tune."

Serving the need is the foundation of our great American system, and figuring out how to do it can make you rich. By the same token, not paying attention to what your customers are saying can destroy your brand.

The great motivational author Norman Vincent Peale wrote, "The trouble with most of us is that we would rather be ruined by praise than saved by criticism."

Being open to feedback, whenever and however it comes at you, digesting it and acting on it, can be a powerful success tool.

Thankfully, I learned this lesson the hard way relatively early in my leadership career. I was managing (not leading) a small group and thought I was doing a great job. One day, my boss called me into his office and presented me with three pages of legal pad with feedback on all the things I was doing wrong as told to him by my team!

I was stunned. But after I got over the shock, I realized that I had not set up effective feedback mechanisms to get course corrections from the people I was being paid to serve.

I went back to the team and wrote all the common points on a flip chart, apologized for being such a poor leader, thanked them profusely for reaching out for help and promised to try to be a better listener going forward.

I also empowered them to give me their candid input immediately and often. Within 12 months I got a promotion.

Bill Gates notes, "Once you embrace unpleasant news, not as a negative but as evidence of a need for change, you aren't defeated by it. You're learning from it."

Here are some tips on how to make sure you are getting the feedback you need.

- Declare to your boss, your peers and those you serve that you are a feedback fanatic. Encourage them to give it to you straight.
- Preserve confidences. The worst feedback killer ever is acting on information in a way that outs the person who gave it to you.

- Have a third party conduct an anonymous annual 360 degree survey, giving your team, your boss and your customers a chance to tell you how effective you are. There are several companies that do this inexpensively and the data you get will be enlightening.

- Collate key feedback points and share them with your team, along with your action plans to improve how you serve. It's best to do this live with your group so that you can ask clarifying questions and respond to additional input.

- Don't be afraid to make a mistake. There are a ton of leadership books out there, but in reality, interpersonal interaction is as much an art as it is a science, especially when you are trying to modify your approach.

- Be open and transparent. When you go down an unproductive path, say so. "I screwed up, I hear you, and I will try to do it differently next time," can be one of the most empowering things you can do.

- In your weekly one-on-ones with direct reports, make sure that the opportunity for feedback exists. "How can I better serve you?" Or, "Is there anything I'm doing that's worrying you," are a couple of good discussion starters.

If you seek feedback with gusto, two things will happen:

By modeling the behavior, you'll eventually create an atmosphere where feedback is welcomed across the organization. People will follow your lead. At first it may be uncomfortable, but folks who don't by in to cultural change have a way of self-selecting out of the organization.

More importantly, you'll become more effective and have more fun. A team that communicates is much more likely to deliver results, work well together and enjoy themselves in the process.

Dick Cavett says, "It's a rare person who wants to hear what he doesn't want to hear."

Be one of those rare people.

Feedback: Its the shortest word in the English language that uses abcdef. It's part of the culture of winning institutions like Google and the Ritz-Carlton. Make it part of your daily bread and you'll quickly get a step closer to where you want to be.

Reinvent Yourself

"The best way to predict your future is to create it!"
– Abraham Lincoln

I had lunch recently with a good friend who is coming to a career crossroads. We met so that he could share his resume with me and brainstorm about opportunities that might fit his background and experience.

It is interesting to watch how these conversations go. Typically, the job seeker has been on Monster.com or has looked at the gigs that are posted in your organization. The lunch is often spent with your friend trying to convince you how to squeeze her skills into what happens to be available.

Contrast that with the Geek Conclaves I have found in the last three cities where we have worked. Talk to them and you will quickly learn that they are doing jobs that did not exist two years ago, let alone when they graduated from college.

"How did you get your current gig?" I would ask.

"I invented it!"

You have read my writing ad nauseum about how important I believe finding your passion is. Life is too short not to be happy, so if you are not happy in your job—a relationship, or where you are living—change it! Chase your joy with reckless abandon. Take responsibility for your own happiness.

Okay, you have heard enough of that. Many of my friends say, that finding that happiness is a lot easier said than done.

True.

If creating your job from scratch, finding a soul mate, or discovering that perfect chalet on 20 acres, with 10MB internet and a Whole Foods down the street were easy, everybody would be doing it.

Happiness requires work, but it is worth the effort.

Germaine Greer writes, "Human beings have an inalienable right to invent themselves.."

That is what my MSUAA co-worker, John Hill, has done. He tells me that the last three positions he has had did not exist before he created them. I believe it. John is a guy who knows exactly what he wants. He has researched it with the enthusiasm of a PHd candidate, and has put together such a compelling pitch that it is impossible not to at least give him a shot at it.

You can do that, too.

Anthony D'angelo says, "If life doesn't offer a game worth playing, then invent a new one." In an economy like ours, where traditional businesses are fighting to stay afloat, CEOs are looking for non-traditional ways to re-think paradigms, find new revenue streams, increase productivity and develop new markets. Think about how you might be able to express your joy in this environment, and let the fun begin.

We may stumble across a million dollar idea, but it is more likely that yours will come after some careful consideration. Ponder these questions:
- When have you been most happy?
- What were you doing then?

- What additional skills, training, relationships and knowledge would you need to become one of the best in the world in that arena?
- How would you sell your idea? What is in it for your potential boss? What is the return on the company's investment in your?
- If someone were to pay you your current salary to prepare for a job you would invent, how would you spend your time preparing?
- How many hours a day would you invest in that preparation?

There are two ways to apply these steps.

The easiest way is to look at the job you currently do. How could you add more value? What are the risks ahead for your organization and how can you be a key player in helping the company deal with them? Where in the chain of command would you like to be in five years and what do you need to do to prepare for it?

We can all take this path anytime we wish. So few people actually think creatively about how they can add more value in their current situation, that those who do are immediately recognized as "keepers".

There is very little competition on the extra mile.

The second way is to begin now, even while you continue at your current assignment, to prepare for the job you want to invent.

Ryan Schram, an MSU grad and the youngest Senior Vice President in the history of the Eprize organization, recommends that you start by giving some spare time to a non-profit organization you believe in. That is a great way to test drive ideas and sharpen skills in an environment where you are very likely to be welcomed with open arms.

See if you can find someone else who is currently doing the thing you would love to do and befriend them. Find out how they prepared, what they did to get the job and how much they are really liking it. Then take a cold, calculated look at how much work and how much fun the thing truly is.

If it is still something that fires your imagination, go for it!

I love Thomas Edison's famous quote, "Opportunity is missed by most people because it is dressed in overalls and looks like work."

So do your homework. And then, make the pitch. Like baseball, the odds of you hitting it out of the park increase with practice and with time at the plate swinging the bat. You will probably strike out the first couple of times you swing, but if you have truly researched the concept and developed yourself into the ideal candidate, eventually you will discover the right environment where you will hit a home run.

Here are some ideas that people thought were crazy a few years ago.

- If your were a traditional banker, would you create a financial service that loaned pennies to the poor in the third world?
- If you were a newspaper, would you offer a service that allows people to advertise goods, services and jobs for free?
- If you were the Encyclopedia Britannica, would you allow readers to contribute and give your content away?

- If you were a radio station, would you allow each listener to put together their own custom playlist and narrowcast it directly to them?

Craig Newmark of Craig's List; Pandora's Tim Westergren; Wikipedia's Jimmie Wales; and Grameen Bank founder, Muhammad Yunus, are among the creative thinkers who turned the prism and re-calibrated our paradigms. They shook the foundations of conventional wisdom in the process and made the world a better place.

There is always opportunity in uncertain times.

Why not chase it?

From a Distance

"You won't comprehend the distance you've traveled until you turn around and realize how far you've been."

When I took the job in suburban Peoria, I knew it would be three months until Colleen and our then very young children could join me. I was house sitting in a cavernous home with just a TV, microwave and a mattress and had, as usual, jumped in way over my head. My days were 18 hours long and as I forced myself NOT to go into the office on weekends, I tried to discover something to take my mind off of how much I was missing my family.

I decided to learn to fly.

My little book, Touch and Go, describes these adventures in greater detail, but my ah-ha moment came the first time I took my little Cessna up solo. As I left the runway at Charlie-15, the buildings, fields, rivers and my earthbound problems got smaller. The intensity of concentration on keeping my plane flying pushed all my worries out of my head. The sensation of solitude, just me and my wings cutting through the mid-winter morning, brought on a feeling of total freedom.

After a time, ideas would begin to fire in my brain. Solutions to long studied problems came up, so many that I started carrying a small tape recorder with me so I could barf them out before forgetting them.

When I would make my final approach and land at our little country airport, I would ponder how this could happen. One moment, the my far-away family and thousands of demanding customers weighed heavily on my shoulders. The next moment it was gone and inspiration began to flow like whitewater.

The renowned publisher Robert G. Collier wrote many years ago about how he approached a challenge. He would write down every fact he could think of about the situation, read it back to himself and then find a quiet chair where he could empty his mind of all conscious thought and let his subconscious work on it. Invariably, an idea would pop out.

We often find ourselves so deep in the weeds of our day-to-day that we totally miss the big picture. The cliche, "missing the forest for the trees" applies here.

Achieving an overarching goal is the result of thousands of little activities and it's easy to focus too intently on the mechanics and forget what you meant to do in the first place.

How, in this world of incredible change, can we make sure we're executing the fundamentals without losing sight on the main objective? Here are some suggestions.

Think about why you're doing all of this. Life is about seeking happiness through service to others. Keep pictures of your loved ones handy to reflect on when you need to get back to your center. Take a break from the day to call your kids, or someone under the age of ten. Youngsters have a way of seeing things as they really are. Listen to the questions they ask you. There is wisdom therein.

Schedule cardiovascular exercise on your calendar at least three times a week and do it! Runners often report that the singularity of focus on putting one foot in front of the other re-charges mind and spirit. The late running guru George Sheehan wrote that our body produces endorphins that are ten times as powerful as morphine. This "runners high" unleashes your mind. Just as he often wrote his columns in his head as he ran, you can take advantage of the extra mental horsepower that cardio provides to put the little behavioral puzzle pieces into the right mental places to keep you pointed toward your goal. "Everyone is an athlete," Sheehan once wrote, "The only difference is that some of us are in training, and some are not."

Empty your mind. Worry is a complete cycle of inefficient thought revolving about a pivot of fear. "Empty your mind of all thoughts. Let your heart be at peace," wrote the Chinese philosopher Lao Tzu. Easier said than done? One pathway to a less burdened brain is through mindfulness. The mindful approach to the simple tasks of your day, washing the dishes for example, can focus your consciousness on what's going on in the present moment. When that happens, the rest of the world can fall into perspective. This can lead to a couple of positive outcomes. First, you'll have some more bandwidth to concentrate effectively on the challenge at hand. Secondly and perhaps more profoundly, whatever the problem, it often becomes lighter. "No human thing is of serious importance," wrote Plato. That might not feel like the truth when your boss is banging you for results, but it is.

When we knew that our time in New Mexico was coming to an end, Colleen and I drove to the top of Sandia Crest. At over eleven thousand feet, the views are staggering. The forest service installed small metal pipes that you could look through to focus on a landmark. The airport, the hospital, our neighborhood, Mount Taylor, the West Mesa, all of these were tiny little circles at the end of a black tunnel. But from a distance they are tiny dots in a beautiful water color painting. A painting that is at once breathtaking and simple, clear and confusing.

So is life.

Julie Gold, a secretary at the HBO cable channel pondered all of this one day and wrote a song that we all know well. Bette Midler still sings it.

From a distance the world looks blue and green,
And the snow-capped mountains white.
From a distance the ocean meets the stream,
And the eagle takes to flight.
From a distance, there is harmony,
And it echoes through the land.
It's the voice of hope, it's the voice of peace,
It's the voice of every man.
If your world seems troubling,
take a look at it – from a distance.

How to be Happy

*"If only we'd stop trying to be happy
we'd have a pretty good time." – Edith Wharton*

My wonderful daughter, Shelby, is one of my biggest cheerleaders. From the time she first understood speech, she heard me talking about how attitude is everything and she practices what I preach.

When she was very young, I loved the times I would tuck her in at bedtime and we would discuss what transpired during each of our days. At the time, Colleen was beginning her pursuit of fitness and Richard Simmons had a daily program on television. Shelby would always start her day's activity list with, "I watched Richard!" Even now, as she turns 30, she still says that if I interrogate her too closely.

Then as now, I was a devotee of the great motivational philosophers and the concept of a "positive mental attitude" was something I tried to teach both Shelby and Brandon early on. I got a lesson in enlightenment one evening when I got ready to turn out her light and asked her, "So, do you remember what PMA is?"

She grinned from ear to ear. She knew the answer!

"Pre-Menstrual Syndrome!"

I struggled with little success in controlling my laughter, "And what does it mean?"

"It means you have to think good thoughts every day of the month!"

When I told Colleen about all of this later, she nodded her head knowingly. "She got it right after all," she said.

Shelby sent me an article from LiveScience.com entitled "The pursuit of happiness is easier said than done."

Science tells us that genetics play a part in our ability to be happy. There is no shame in being aware that you may be clinically depressed, and the cadre of medications available in that realm can truly change lives.

But psychologist Sonja Lyubomirsky of the University of California, Riverside told LiveScience Senior Writer Clara Moskovitz that, "Despite the finding that happiness is partially genetically determined, and despite the finding that life situations have a smaller influence on our happiness than we think they do, we argue that still a large portion of happiness is in our power to change."

51 studies reviewed by Lyumbomirsky and her colleagues tested attempts to increase happiness through different types of positive thinking. The results, published in the Journal of Clinical Psychology, point to five things you can do to be happier.

- Be grateful: Some study participants were asked to write letters of gratitude to people who had helped them in some way. The study found that these people reported a lasting increase in happiness over weeks and even months after implementing the habit. What's even more surprising: Sending the letter is not necessary. Even when people wrote letters but never delivered them to the addressee, they still reported feeling better afterwards.

- **Be optimistic:** Another practice that seems to help is optimistic thinking. Study participants were asked to visualize an ideal future (for example, living with a loving and supportive partner, or finding a job that was fulfilling) and describe the image in a journal entry. After doing this for a few weeks, these people too reported increased feelings of well-being.
- **Count your blessings:** People who practice writing down three good things that have happened to them every week show significant boosts in happiness studies have found. It seems the act of focusing on the positive helps people remember reasons to be glad.
- **Use your strengths:** Another study asked people to identify their greatest strengths, and then to try to use these strengths in new ways. For example, someone who says they have a good sense of humor could try telling jokes to lighten up business meetings or cheer up sad friends. This habit, too, seems to heighten happiness.
- **Commit acts of kindness:** It turns out helping others also helps ourselves. People who donate time or money to charity, or who altruistically assist people in need, report improvements in their own happiness.

Dr. Lyubomirsky has taken the art of happiness to the iPhone, creating an application, called Live Happy, to help people boost their well-being.

Elizabeth Scott is a PHd candidate at San Diego State. She writes about stress for about.com. Scott recommends learning the art of "reframing".

"Reframing," Scott says, "is a way of changing the way you look at something and, thus, changing your experience of it. Reframing can turn a stressful event into either a major trauma or a challenge to be bravely overcome. Reframing can depict a really bad day as a mildly low point in an overall wonderful life. Reframing can see a negative event as a learning experience. Reframing is a way that we can alter our perceptions of stressors and, thus, relieve significant amounts of stress and create a more positive life before actually making any changes in our circumstances."

Reframing works because your body can't tell the difference between real stress and perceived stress. From Scott's February 15th About.com essay, here are four techniques to help you learn to reframe.

- **Learn About Thinking Patterns.** The first step in reframing is to educate yourself about some of these negative thinking patterns that may exacerbate your stress levels. See these common cognitive distortions to see which ones, if any, may come into play in your life. Also, read about negative explanatory styles to learn the particular way that pessimists view their life experiences; since pessimists tend to experience more stress and less success than do optimists, it's important to understand how they think, and work to adopt a positive explanatory style instead. Educating yourself about thinking patterns and how they affect people is important for laying the groundwork for understanding and change.

- **Notice Your Thoughts.** The next step is to catch yourself when you're slipping into overly negative and stress-inducing patterns of thinking. Being aware of them is an important part of challenging and ultimately changing them. One thing you can do is just become more mindful of your thoughts, as though you are an observer. When you catch negative thinking styles, just note them at first. If you want, you can even keep a journal and start recording what's happening in your life and your thoughts surrounding these events, and then examine these thoughts through your new 'lens' to get more practice in catching these thoughts. Another helpful practice is meditation, where you learn to quiet your mind and examine your thoughts. Once you become more of an observer, it is easier to notice your thoughts rather than remaining caught up in them.

- Challenge Your Thoughts. As you notice your negative thoughts, an effective part of reframing involves examining the truth and accuracy (or lack thereof) of these thoughts. Are the things you are telling yourself even true? Also, what are some other ways to interpret the same set of events? Which ways of seeing things serve you better? Instead of seeing things the way you always have, challenge every negative thought and see if you can adopt thoughts that fit your situation but reflect a more positive outlook.

- Replace Your Thoughts With More Positive Thoughts. Have you even been to a hospital and noticed that the nurses often ask people about their 'discomfort' rather than their 'pain'? That's reframing in action. If the patient is in searing pain, the term 'discomfort' becomes annoying and seems to reflect a disconnect in understanding, but if the pain is mild, reframing it as 'discomfort' can actually minimize the experience of pain for many patients. This is a useful reframing trick that we can all put into practice. When you are looking at something negative, see if you can change your self talk to use less strong, less negative emotions. When you are looking at a potentially stressful situation, see if you can view it as a challenge vs. a threat. Look for the 'gift' in each situation and see if you can see your stressors on the more positive edge of reality: see them in a way that still fits the facts of your situation, but that is less negative and more optimistic and positive.

With these skills in your happiness toolbox you can discover how to change your life by changing how you look at life.

Are You in Sync with Your Boss?

"When I want your advice, I'll tell you what it is!"

Years ago (and I do mean years ago), I earned my first Vice President gig. Among my direct reports was a manager who everyone thought was a golden boy, a man who seemed to do everything right, a rising star. I was excited to meet him.

Almost from the start, things went wrong. I would say that something was "blue" and he would argue that, "No, it's blue!" He was a very able guy, but we just could not get in sync. He went on to a great leadership career and we are still good friends, but it was my first experience with team chemistry.

One of the things I've always done when working on a key hire is to put together an interview team. The team is made up of peers and also includes a few of the key people he or she will serve. Some would call these folks subordinates, but in my upside down view of the world, the closer you are to the customer, the more important you are to the organization.

The team interviewed each candidate, one to one, and we would gather afterward and debrief. There were three questions I asked:

- What were the candidate's strengths.
- What were the candidate's weaknesses.
- How would the candidate fit into the team and the culture we are trying to build?

That last one is the chemistry question. For an organization to thrive, there has to be the right chemistry. We don't all have to agree, but we all have to be willing to work together toward a common objective. We have to trust one another and base the relationship on a candid, no bullshit accountability, where we all help one another be the best we can be and model the behavior.

When you work for a boss, you may not always have the luxury of having the chemistry you would like. But the two of you can agree on "rules of engagement" that will make the partnership productive.

Barry Robertson, in his superb High Impact Leadership Seminar for the Stop at Nothing organization, teaches that we all come to a relationship with a point of view and our own unique communication styles. The more we can understand others points of view and com-munication styles, the more effective we can be as leaders, peers and team members.

In some companies, everybody takes the Myers Briggs Indicator, which can help us understand likely behaviors. At one assignment, my team used to request that we put our Myers Briggs type on our name badges instead of our job titles. "Hello, I'm Scott Westerman – ENTJ".

I can still hear them now, "Oh No! Here comes another Intuitive Extrovert. Head for the exits!"

Even if your company doesn't put your personality type on your badge, here's an excellent way to get in sync with your boss. It can work whether you've just started a new reporting relationship, or have been working together for several years.

Jill Geisler heads the Leadership and Management Group at The Poynter Institute. She works with managers at every level of print, broadcast and online news organizations, helping them become more effective leaders. Jill developed a useful tool you and your boss can use to sync up on the most important dimensions of your working relationship.

She calls it "Twenty Questions about Your Boss"

Her web page at Poynter provides some illuminating insights on why managing your boss can be good for both of you. Quoting:

Managing your boss means:
- Knowing her work habits and how they affect you.
- Communicating in ways he's most likely to hear.
- Recognizing her values and looking for alignment.
- Representing your staff's wins, concerns or needs effectively.
- Building trust that makes successes more enjoyable and failures less than fatal.
- Anticipating his needs, so you can plan your work/ manage your time accordingly.
- Knowing how to disagree constructively; as the loyal opposition, not just the opposition.
- Ensuring "a place at the table" for your team, when many others in the organization are requesting resources.
- Helping one another through knowledge of each other's strengths and weaknesses.
-

In truth, Jill is also talking about how to effectively manage your team. So if YOU are a boss, perhaps taking this 20 question quiz can help improve you and your team's performance too.

Twenty Questions about Your Boss:
- Preferred method of giving info to me:

- Preferred method of getting info from me:
- Biggest current pressure:
- Stands for these values, first and foremost:
- Biggest "hot button":
- Passion outside of work:
- Has expertise in:
- Lacks expertise in:
- Vision for our organization:
- Would be really hurt if someone:
- Best boss my boss ever worked for:
- Expects this from me when there's a small problem:
- Expects this from me then there's a big problem:
- Will not compromise when it comes to:
- Considers a great day at work to be:
- Handles pressure by:
- Is respected by her/his bosses for:
- Respects others for:
- Has a blind spot about:
- Thinks I'm great at:

How did it go? How do you imagine your boss would answer these questions about you? How would you answer the questions about yourself?

I know one manager who took the test and shared his answers with his entire team, "Just so you know what to expect from me." He asked each team member to fill out one for themselves. He used it during performance reviews to help set goals, and keeps the tests in a binder on his desk so he can tailor his communication style based on a "middle ground that is true to who I am as a leader, and true to who they are as leaders."

Some economists are predicting that 20% of us will change jobs in 2010.

If you are one of them, getting in sync can make all the difference.

The Illusion of Stability
and the Joy of Doing

"I have realized that the past and future are real illusions,
that they exist in the present,
which is what there is and all there is." – Alan Watts

When Colleen and I visited Hawaii, one of the first places we explored was the famed Waimea Bay. The Beach Boys sang about it in "Surfin' USA" and I wanted to see, up close, how those boys and girls "with their feet full of tar and their full of sand" attacked the rollers.

They make it look easy, but it is not.

Back in the late 60s, I spent summers at Port Sheldon on Lake Michigan. We had long boards then, and if the wind was right, the Big Lake could swirl up some significant surf.

We had to paddle out against an incredible power that was trying to press us back to shore. When we finally got out to that place where waves are born, we scanned the churning waters for the subtle signs of what might be a good wave to ride. Once we had selected one, it was a weird combination of art and science to catch it. You have to paddle for just the right time, stand up just as the wave crests and hold your balance while you did your best to ride it in, in style.

Sometimes the wave would turn out to be a dud. Sometimes you did not time it right and it passed you by. Sometimes you got there too fast and would slide over the crest and roll in discomfort and danger in the depths of Mother Nature's blender. Even if you caught the crest, it was oh so easy to lose your balance and fall before you finished the ride. If you are doing all of this at Waimea Bay, another dimension is added: Sharks. Ask Bethany Hamilton about that interesting distraction.

So it is with life.

The direction, location and power of the waves change. New predators (competitors) emerge. Surfboard technology improves, and surfers re-invent every step of the process, all in pursuit of the perfect ride on the perfect wave.

This is happening at many companies right now. Products with a unique selling proposition are becoming commoditized. Revenues may not be growing as fast as they used to. And many firms have to totally reinvent themselves to better ride the waves.

I got an up-close-and-personal feel for this when I was charged with consolidating one of our outposts recently. It included the elimination of positions for a number of folks, some who had ridden the waves of change with us for 20 years plus.

Together, we went through all the stages of grief and a common theme was, "This was such a stable job. We are doing so well, why does it have to change?"

These surfers had not been watching the water. As the competition heats up, more surfers want to ride the same wave. New technologies are calming the revenue waters at our beach and making waves up the street. And all along, we were surfing the same beach with the same gear at the same time, expecting a great ride.

Talk to any elite athlete or successful business person and they will tell you that there is no such thing as stability. Needs change. Products and services come and go. And life is a constant exercise in re-invention.

The waves are always changing so we need to change too. As employees, we're the surfers. The company is our surfboard. Our competitors are the sharks and the marketplace is the wave.

We need to constantly be scanning the ocean to figure out which market has that magical combination of profitability and joy that makes for a great career day. We need to choose our surf boards carefully. They should be well built and well designed to ride the waves we choose. We need to develop our skills, stamina and attitude so that we are able to jump on the board and ride the waves as best as we can, learning from our wipe outs, and not getting too confident that one good ride will instantly produce another.

I have never learned how to pronounce Mihaly Csikszent-mihalyi's name, but his masterwork is a book called *Flow*. He dispels the common myth that the destination is what life is all about. Behave and you will get candy. Do well on your tests and you will earn a degree. M.C. believes that it is the journey, not the destination, where the true joy of living resides.

Have you ever felt a moment of exuberance when you are in the middle of doing something that you really love? Colleen says that I am "in the zone", when immersed in the nuances of a spreadsheet formula, or working on recording a new song on my multi-track recording gear. Long distance runners report the same thing when the endorphins kick in and it feels like they could run forever.

According to Wikipedia, flow is "a single-minded immersion and represents perhaps the ultimate in harnessing the emotions in the service of performing and learning. In flow the emotions are not just contained and channeled, but positive, energized, and aligned with the task at hand. The hallmark of flow is a feeling of spontaneous joy, even rapture, while performing a task."

If you have been in that state, you know what it is like and you seek more opportunities to spend time there.

The good news is, that you can get to that space even if your company takes away your surfboard. Here are the steps:

First, think about what really makes you happy. When you felt the Flow state, what were you doing? What job would you do if you were already rich and working for love and not for money?

Once you have figured that out (and as your life progresses your joy may change), think about how you can manifest it. Talk to people who are in that space. How did they get there? What skills to they have? Who do they interact with?

Then, begin to act like the person who already has what you seek. How do they dress? What behaviors do they develop? How do they deal with failure? Where do they live? What do they drive? What fitness plan do they have? How have they visualized where they want to be five years from now and what goals have they set to get there?

Earl Nightingale's wise maxim, "We become what we think about," is the key here. Act now as the person you would like to become and you WILL become that person.

This is a powerful thing, so be careful. It's as easy to become a failure as it is to become a success. Get stuck in negative emotions, defeatist attitudes and feelings of unworthiness and you will attract like people and become unworthy.

So think positive thoughts, look for opportunity amidst challenges. And develop habits and relationships that can help you become the person you want to be.

Companies and jobs don't have futures. People do.

The wave and the surfboard don't feel the Joy. The surfer does.

So enjoy the ride.

Helping the Competition

"An able competitor can inspire our best work."

Once upon a time, I was in line for a promotion. I was in the middle of my grueling preparation routine when I got a call from a co-worker. "Full disclosure," he said, "I wanted you to know that we are both competing for the same promotion."

We are friends. He said he didn't want me to hear about it from someone else. I thought that was a classy thing to do.

Then I got a crazy idea.

"You know, both of us have strengths that could help the other during the interview process. Why don't we prep each other so we can both can do our best?"

That sounds nuts on the surface. Why would you want to help a competitor win the job you desire? And why would anyone else who is competing with you even consider sharing his secrets?

My friend didn't miss a beat, "That's a terrific idea. Lets do it!"

We spent the next hour sharing nuggets from our areas of expertise, talking about how we would approach the job, sometimes debating the validity of an idea, but all the time trying to better understand the value that each other brought to the table.

What followed was an email chain. I sent him the spreadsheets that helped me track progress, and explained sales strategies and my favorite management techniques. He sent me a blizzard of details on a section of the business where his expertise is nationally recognized.

We agreed that our joint goal was to help the company hire the best possible person for the gig and realized that, no matter how the chips fell, we would each enjoy working for the other.

I told my team members about the encounter. Some may have thought that their boss was crazy, but there was an interesting gleam in the eyes of others.

That gleam made sense to me two weeks later, when I learned that three of them were applying to succeed me in the role I was about to relinquish.

Naturally, I helped each of them prep for their first interview encounter. I know them well and shot tough questions their way, gave them feedback on their answers and tried to share the lessons I had learned in the role. It was enthralling to watch. them work things through and gratifying to see that some of the ideas I had tried to teach them over our time together had taken root.

But the real surprise came later. I saw two of them heading out together at the lunch hour. When I asked what they were doing they said, "We are sharing our knowledge with one another so that we can both be our best during the interview process."

It turned out that all three of them had spontaneously agreed to help one another prepare.

Clearly, this approach only works if you have built a team who trust one another and are genuinely able to put the best interests of the group first. They have worked hard over time to build a unique bond. In our staff meetings, everyone pitches in to understand and assist with an individual's challenge, even if its technically outside of their core competency. Sometimes, the best technical solutions came from our call center guy. And our marketing lead offered to off load some of the finance person's work so that we could hit a forecast and customer communication deadline on time.

I can't yet tell you who will get the two jobs that my buddy and I, and my three extraordinary team members are competing for. But my sense is that the likelihood of the right person being selected has gone up substantially.

Because we are all in it together.

Are You Between Opportunities? Make the Most of It!

"You must do the things you think you cannot do."
– Eleanor Roosevelt

The big, scary question that confronts anybody who has lost a job is: What do I do now?

If you have been paying any attention to the economic news, you have probably already developed a Plan-B. How do I live more frugally? How big is my rainy day fund? What is my back-up plan for revenue generation while I figure out what is next? Smart people have already had that conversation with their financial advisers and have been working their professional networks, building the relationships they will need tomorrow – now.

If it really happens, if you get the word that your services are no longer needed at your current place of employment, how do you make the most of that time when you are "between opportunities."

Sharpen the Saw: That's my favorite of Stephen Covey's Seven Habits of Highly Effective People. Use your hiatus as a chance to learn a new skill. Expand your knowledge of the issues and talents you will need when you get back on your career track. Go to Borders and load up on books. Buy the caffeinated beverage of your choice at the coffee bar, find a quiet corner and fill your brain. Take a class. Get that license or certification you have been thinking about. Write a book. Get fit.

Re-calibrate your Joy: This topic deserves its own blog post, but here is the Reader's Digest Condensed version. Scott's First Life Life law is this: Life is about seeking your joy and chasing it with reckless abandon. Push the fear into a box, go someplace where you can get inspired (the ocean, the mountains, the desert) take out a legal pad and start to dream. If you could take a success pill that would ensure that you would be a smash in whatever you did, what would that job look like? Journal what a typical day would look like in that world. Where do you live, who do you work with, what additional education and experience have you had, where do you work out, what car are you driving, what do you eat? Paint as vivid a picture as you can. Then study which companies have the job you want, pick the one that best fits your values, research their competitors, think of ways you can help them add value in these challenging times, figure out what is currently stopping you from getting that dream gig, then prepare and go for it.

Give Yourself Away: Here is another one of Scott's Life Laws: Great servants are ultimately great leaders. If you are re-inventing yourself, find a way to test drive your new skills and habits. If you are a marketing major who has been stuck in a gig that is outside of your area of education, find a hungry non-profit and go offer yourself as their marketing director – for free. Give them 60 intensive days of hard work. Help them clarify their mission and vision. Improve their marketing strategies and tactics. Reach out to people who can help them with the execution. In essence, you are doing the job. You will be interacting in that world, building a network and a reputation. If you have any success at all, it is an instant resume item. Whatever your passion, there are ways that you can give it away and learn a ton in the process. By the way, you can do this even if you've taken another 'emergency' job as a stop-gap.

Nurture your Most Important Relationships: Catch up with a few of those important people that Keith Ferrazzi talks about in Never Eat Alone. You have got the time. Figure out how you can help them take some additional steps toward their dreams. DO NOT write one of those "How are you? I'm out of work and need help" emails, especially if you have been lax in communicating in the past. One of the magical things about giving unselfishly is that it ultimately pays back exponentially.

Have Faith: Just about every person that has ever left my team has ended up in a better situation. Just recently I heard from a young woman that "self selected" out of our organization. She told me that, "Getting fired turned out to be a good thing. It forced me to do what I've been wanting to do for a long time." Not everybody will feel this when they are in the uncomfortable moment, but if you look at the event as an opportunity to jump off of your career plateau, exiting your current job could be the best thing that ever happened to you.

Energy Suckers

"If people around you aren't going anywhere, if their dreams are no bigger than hanging out on the corner, or if they're dragging you down, get rid of them. Negative people can sap your energy so fast, and they can take your dreams from you, too." That is MSU's Earvin Johnson talking about energy suckers.

You know the type, the drama queens and complainer kings, those high maintenance people in your life who are quick to criticize and slow to act, first to spread gossip and last to take personal accountability.

Energy suckers see every day as a bad day. The best they can do when you ask how it is going is to say, "It's going." They need endless financial and emotional support and are insensitive to everybody else.

Who are the energy suckers in your life? There is an easy test. What people make you cringe when you get a text message or email from them? Who makes you instinctively press the "forward to voice mail" button when their number pops up on your caller ID? Who makes your chest tighten whenever they enter a room and you exhale whenever they leave?

These are the people that author Phylameana Lila Desey calls "psychic vampires." "They are not bad people," she writes, "Most of them are not aware on a conscious level that they are

125

doing what they are doing. Still, their unknowing actions can play havoc...The harm in a psychic attack is that there is no fair exchange of energy and therefore one feels depleted while the other becomes energized."

Our personal energy is the true coin of the realm. It is a limited resource and we have to invest it carefully. While energy suckers are always a part of the world we inhabit, how we deal with them will impact both our productivity and our happiness.

We have all heard the classic advice, change the things you can change, accept the things you can't change. There's a third alternative that applies to energy suckers:

Remove yourself from the unacceptable.

I got an email from my good friend and long time colleague, Diane Villegas, the other day. The company where she worked was evolving away from a place where she felt the joy of contribution. The new regime didn't share her priorities and the extra hours she formerly was glad to contribute were becoming less rewarding.

I've always loved Diane's approach to here career. Her lifestyle required a well paying gig, but she'll chuck a job in a nano-second if it isn't in sync with who she is.

Her note had the following subject line:

"I removed myself from the unacceptable."

We are judged by the company we keep and, invariably, that company can influence who we are. So minimize the time with the negative people in your life.

If you find yourself stuck in an interaction with an energy sucker, recognize the moments when that person is in vampire mode and don't give up your power. I once heard a co-worker tell an energy sucker, "I'm sorry that you feel the way you do, but I can't be dragged into this."

This stunned the vampire, who immediately went into guilt-trip mode, "So what you're saying is that you won't help me?"

My co-worker responded gently but firmly, "You have to help yourself."

Sounds pretty direct, and it is. But as Road Less Traveled author M. Scott Peck once wrote, "The only way to stop a behavior is to stop it."

The truth is, we all need the benefit of someone else's energy from time to time. That is normal and that is what friends are for.

In healthy relationships one plus one equals three where energy is concerned. Even if you are feeling down, a little time with that other person make you both feel stronger.

If you've ever been in a room with a group of high energy people who are working on a problem together, the obstacles have a way of becoming manageable. Even if only make a modicum of progress is made, everybody walks away feeling great.

So do your best to surround yourself with people who have dreams, goals and a game plan. Hang with people who are good listeners, who are not afraid to give you candid feedback and who model the behaviors to which you aspire.

And when you see an energy sucker coming your way, cross the street.

Those with whom we associate, we become.

Be Brief

"If it takes a lot of words to say what you have in mind, give it more thought." – Dennis Roth

---

Sometimes I get on a roll. As I research my Monday missives I admit to occasions when I have so much I want to share that some readers with normal pre-caffeinated attention spans don't quite have the stamina to keep up.

Such was the feedback I heard from a beloved colleague after she read my chapter on energy suckers. So I've tried to learn to be brief.

I had the good fortune to be on the same platform with a number of politicians during my executive years. I had the honor of introducing our then mayor and realized that I knew very little about him. I grabbed his shoulder just before showtime and asked how he would like to be introduced.

"There's no such thing as a bad short speech," he said, "or a good long speech."

That was the extent of the background he shared with me. So I marched up to the microphone and said, "Ladies and Gentlemen, Mayor Richard Austin!"

And so it goes with much of our business and personal communications these days.

All problems on TV resolve themselves in less then 58 minutes. You are lucky to get a 25 second sound byte on the local news.

Cell phones and Twitter have further sensitized us to getting our message across in 140 characters or less.

The reality is that the biggest challenges defy the oversimplification that our 24 hour news cycle and micro-attention spans require.

That being said, there is a lot we can do to "get to the point".

If you are writing an email, be aware that most people scan their inboxes by way of the message pane in Outlook. If you can not get your point across in the paragraph that is visible there, it is highly unlikely that your reader will scroll down to see what is "below the fold."

Same goes for voice mail. My cable co-workers used to say that, "Scott gives your 15 seconds to get his attention, then he deletes your voice mail."

Sad but true. I remember a call center manager saving an important action item until the last part of her phone message. I never got that far.

When you present to a client or co-worker, think of that same mind set. We love executive summaries that give us the key nuggets to chew on. And we feel the Ambien kicking in when the deck has 20 or more pages in it.

I used to require an overly PowerPoint verbose VP to put everything he wanted to tell me on no more than two slides. He did, but he also included a ten page appendix with graphs and charts to amplify his points.

Many of the problems we face are complex, but we can often quickly identify an activity we can begin immediately to attack them.

"I would like to give you a quick overview of what is in front of us today and will then share two things we will do to move the needle."

Those intros are music to my ears.

So as you think about that presentation, that speech, that interaction, remember the seven magic words:

"Be brief, be brilliant and be gone!"

Arrogance and Complacency

*"When a great team loses through complacency,
it will constantly search for new and more intricate explanations
to explain away defeat." – Pat Riley*

I rode Amtrak into Chicago to spend the day with Jana O'Brien. We first met at Michigan State when I was spending to much time on the radio and she was building the fundamentals of a brilliant career in advertising research.

We contemplated our reflections in Cloudgate, that incredible sliver space ship at Millennium Park, and she told me about her fascinating conversation with Don Keough, then president of Coca Cola. At age 81, he wrote The Ten Commandments of Business Failure, which postulates that "You learn more from your mistakes than from your successes."

Two things mark the imminent decline of a brand, he said: Arrogance and complacency.

"It is very easy for people who are associated with great brands to be arrogant," he told Jana, "because when you are associated with a great company and a great brand, the people just automatically endow you with a little bit more wisdom than you are entitled to have, and they give a little more deference than you deserve."

With regard to competitors, Keough says, "You hope that they are good, because they can keep the virus of complacency, out of your system. I used to say that if the Pepsi Cola Company didn't exist, we'd just had to invent it, because we knew that there was always somebody breathing down our neck."

That's a mouthful.

As I rode the train back to East Lansing the irony set in. These same rails were at one time the conduits of progress and the main mode of transcontinental transport. They may still transport commerce across the land, but are a shadow of their former dominance.

Arrogance and complacency played a role.

Markets change, innovations abound. And yet, we often chain ourselves to our current reality long past the moment when we need to adjust.

When I visited EPrize a short time back, one of the many quotes plastered on the walls of the converted brewery they call home hit me right between the eyes.

"Somebody is going to put us out of business. It might as well be us."

That was written by EPrize's founder and CEO, Josh Linkner.

Here is an organization at the top of its game, already planning their own demise and renaissance.

What can we learn from American passenger railroads, from Michigan's economic challenges, and from the gyrations in each of the companies with whom we temporarily share our personal brand?

- **Know thy customer:** Our market is diverse and fickle, but we can discover what they need and what motivates them to act. We can determine what relationships are profitable, what relationships are not and build strategies and tactics accordingly. Most of all, we can realize that what they want tomorrow will be different than what they want today.

- **Serve thy customer:** Remember always that careers, love affairs, business and life are all about relationships. Relationships are multidimensional and fluid. They require constant attention and nurturing. You must re-earn your stripes every day. You can not bank a marriage on the Internet alone and nothing beats face to face.

- **Anticipate:** Arrogance and complacency are based on the assumption that you are too big to fail and will always be the market leader. In truth, people are always re-evaluating the return on their investment. Whether it is a cell phone company or a mortgage, there is a point where they will walk away. Develop a sixth sense for what your customers will want tomorrow and do it today.

- **Innovate or die:** Just as your customer's needs change, so must you change to meet them. Markets saturate. New alternatives emerge. Your competition will likely change. And if you are currently at the head of the pack, you are in the cross hairs of everyone who is behind you. Expand your knowledge, add to your tool box. And do not be afraid to disconnect your personal brand from the organization if its becoming arrogant and complacent.

None of this should frighten you. Change is a natural law that is as old as time. In the depths of the darkest night lies the promise of a new day.

So stay humble. As Einstein says, "Whoever undertakes to set himself up as a judge of Truth and Knowledge is shipwrecked by the laughter of the gods."

Do your best to embrace change. As your humble servant has so written, "They who can anticipate change and adjust are most likely to profit from it.

Rivalries

One of my earliest football memories is being a Boy Scout usher at Michigan Stadium on the day when Michigan State came to town. Then as now, the U of M regular season was a run-up to the Ohio State game and Bump Elliot, Bo Schembechler, et al, always hoped that they could escape their encounter with the Spartans of East Lansing to prepare for the annual event that often determined who would go to the Rose Bowl.

Sitting on the hard concrete steps of the "Hole that Yost dug, Chrysler paid for and Canham carpeted," I contemplated the 101,001 fans in attendance. Half wore Wolverine Maize and Blue and half wore Spartan Green and White. All were cheering at the top of their combined lungs. It was the World Cup with vocal chords instead of those damned soccer horns. It did not stop from the time the teams came on the field, until the last second had ticked off of the clock.

It was said on both sides of the gridiron that no matter how bad or good either team might have been before that particular Saturday, when MSU met U of M, it was anybody's ballgame.

Such is the energy surrounding a rivalry.

When I was new to my Comcast job in Albuquerque, a reporter for the local business weekly asked me what I thought about our team competing with QWest, the local old-school phone company.

My response is still used in Comcast's public relations training as the essence of the inappropriate answer:

"I can't wait to get into their lunch box and fight over the red meat."

Truth is, competition is that "rising tide that lifts all boats." When it is healthy, it fosters continuous improvement in the quality to value quotient in a way that benefits everyone concerned.

But the benefits of a great rivalry are often perverted by those who descend into dogmatic dismemberment of the other side. Colleen and I were in a restaurant in Ann Arbor sometime back. When the proprietor learned we were Spartans (I tell everybody), he began a five minute diatribe of tired and discredited shots at the institution.

Some of this is normal. We would not be good team players if we did not poke some fun at the competition with some regularity. I have been known to say that, "When you see someone wearing Green and White, you know they went to Michigan State, but when you see someone in Maize and Blue, they could have gone to WalMart." In this instance, it became clear to me that this particular individual was so attached to his team that anyone who supported someone else was a heretic.

I felt sorry for him. Colleen said, flat out, that we weren't eating there ever again.

Contrast this to my experience in the Land of the Wolverines this past Saturday. The one person that everyone in Ann Arbor wants to talk to is Lucy Ann Lance. Along with her long time radio partner, Dean Erskine, she interviews the great and near great about things that are important to them. Her interest is so genuine and her questions so carefully crafted that she and Dean have built a hugely loyal following in the community.

Like many, she found it mildly fascinating that a kid who literally grew up in the shadow of the Big House would become such a passionate evangelist for the U of M's chief rival. So she invited me to come down and talk with her about it.

I thought a lot about the message I wanted to share that day and it came down to this:

The competition between our two Universities makes us both stronger. But if we are to return the State of Michigan, and our Nation to it's rightful place as the innovation engine for the world, we have to do it together.

Ben Franklin's message to the Continental Congress that, "We must all hang together, or assuredly we shall all hang separately," has real meaning for all of us who associate our personal brand with any organization.

The most abundance goes to they who create abundance for others. We can not do it alone.

This was brought into clear focus for me when Colleen was diagnosed with cancer late last year, right around the time we were returning to our home state. We instantly wanted the best care we could find. The Cancer Center at the University of Michigan was where we wanted to be.

I regularly wore my Spartan armor when I accompanied Colleen to A2 for chemotherapy. Despite our clear academic alliances, we were both effusive in our gratitude that these exceptional Wolverine doctors were on the case.

The nurses in the infusion center got to know us well, and one day, when I was saying how much I appreciated Michigan medical care, a nurse pointed to the bag of clear liquid that was slowly dripping into Colleen's IV, "We have some great docs here, but the drug that is saving her life was invented at MSU."

She was referring to Carboplatin, the real life miracle drug that Michigan State University scientists revealed as an effective cancer killer.

All this was on my mind as I told Lucy Ann:

You can't have Green grass without a Blue sky.

Ann Arbor doctors save more lives thanks to East Lansing medicine.

Michigan Football Coach Bo Schembechler and Michigan State Basketball Coach Tom Izzo have, together, transformed the definition of student athlete excellence.

And the next renaissance here in the Great Lakes State will be energized by Michigan and Michigan State together.

Whatever it is that you do, whatever team you root for, it is okay to be proud. It is okay to put lots of points on your side of the board. Winning sure fells a lot better than losing. Remember, too, how competition has made you a stronger

139

person, and that healthy rivalries ultimately elevate the quality of the game...

For everyone.

Making Others Aware
of Your Potential

"Imagine yourself as if you already were
what you potentially could be.
Demonstrate it to others every day
and you will become that person."

The Snyder/Phillips Gallery sets the standard for residence hall dining at Michigan State University. With food stations named New Traditions, Latitudes, The Berg, Ciao, The Brimstone Grille and Bliss, you immediately get the sensation that this is no ordinary culinary experience.

Whenever I have visitors on Campus, I try to put a SnyPhi meal on the schedule. And on the rare occasions when I eat lunch alone, I love to bask in the energy that emanates there.

And so it was that I took a respite from MSUAA's Grandparents University week for some Tofu Wellington, the usual piled high Berg salad bar creation and a couple of slices of Hawaiian pizza.

I wear my MSUAA name badge just about everywhere. It is a subconscious invitation to conversation and friendship. That is how I met Denise Zieleniewski.

She is the first in her family to go to college and a role model for a procession of siblings, nieces and nephews who are following in her academic footsteps. She is the head HR servant for the MSU Residential and Hospitality Services division.

But her career did not start at that level.

As I guzzled my glass of chocolate milk (mixed with skim) she casually threw out another inspiring piece of advice.

Learn how to make others aware of your potential.

As the chief executive officer in charge of your personal brand, you have probably come to realize that there is no direct path to any career goal. It is a constant mixture of continuous education, exploration and exposition.

That last word, "exposition", is another way of saying that it is up to us to market our brand.

The first step is good preparation. Once you have identified your passion, build the skills, experience and network you need to move in that environment.

The second step is effective execution. Whatever your current role, work it to perfection. Deliver on your objectives with professionalism, a smile and a positive attitude.

The third step is where most people falter. Put yourself in situations where others can become aware of your potential. Here are some ideas that can help.

Present: Offer to be the face and the voice of your department in presentations to other sections of your operation. Our exceptional marketing director at Comcast Albuquerque first caught my attention as a manager when presented an overview of the department's marketing plan to the business unit leadership team.

- **Pitch in:** There are always things happening in every organization that require an extra set of hands. Helping out in another area is a great way to make new friends, get exposed to new skills and ideas, and further bracket your passion.

- **Volunteer:** Over the course of a recent week, I had the honor of attending three separate mega events that MSUAA sponsors across the State. I'm always on the lookout for new talent and potential leaders at these things and I am never disappointed. Often it is one of my friends that points out that hard worker that popped above the radar for the first time.

- **Ask thoughtful questions:** One or our interns approached me on his first day in the seat and said, "I've noticed that a couple of our processes seem confusing to the team. Have you seen the same thing?"

- **Share ideas for improvement:** In the next breath, the intern gave me some interesting solutions based on his experience in another department. I now use him as a regular sounding board.

I am certain that Denise did all of these things and more to earn the ability to express her joy as a senior leader on Team MSU. What other ways can you think of to help make others aware of your potential?

Blooming Where You Are Planted

"Our True Home Is Within."

The other day, my friend Kathleen reminded me of the spiritual maxim, "Bloom where you are planted." She is a shining example.

After relocating with her young child, she discovered that the teaching career she had planned on was not materializing. Rather than abandoning her home base, she pondered what opportunities might lie right their in the neighborhood. Thinking carefully about that magic point where her passions intersected with her skills, she took her Michigan State University education and focused it on becoming a free lance editor. To shorten a long story (most success does not happen overnight), she now can pick her clients, is loving where she is living and earns the income to enjoy the fruits of her labors.

Each year I have the good fortune to attend the pre-event for the 12th annual Steve Smith charity golf outing. It is always inspiring to hear Steve talk, especially so this time as our other special guest was Spartan for Life, Tom Izzo. But the most interesting conversation I had at the most recent gathering was with another former Spartan athlete. He is a Great Lakes Stater by birth and has leveraged his academic achievement and his athletic notoriety to build a successful business career. He felt the call to return to where he was originally planted. He is reinventing himself in Michigan as an example to others who might be considering up-rooting.

True, geographic flexibility increases your chance of hitting striking gold, but do not be afraid to look for your acres of diamonds in your own back yard.

Ask yourself these questions:

- What do you most enjoy doing?
- What un-met needs are there in the area where you now live?
- What additional skills, education, contacts and resources do you need to connect your passion with a value proposition?

Ray Croc was a milkshake mixer salesman who started making hamburgers when he saw how they helped increase his sales volume. That became the genesis of the McDonald's story. The bicycle couriers you see racing between the congressional office buildings in Washington began as a single kid who found himself stuck in DC with a bike and the need for some income.

In truth, opportunity exists wherever you are if you spread your field of view wide enough to recognize it.

This also applies to whatever job you are now doing. Look at the big picture. Understand how your work and the work of your department contributes to the larger goals of the organization. Sometimes, re-engineering the way the work is done, teaching the current team some new skills, or simply providing a little energizing cheerleading can take the operation and your career to an entirely new level.

One of the reasons I deeply believe that Michigan will recover and thrive in this new century is embodied in our State motto:

"Si Quaeris Peninsulam Amoenam Circumspice." – "If you seek a pleasant peninsula, look about you."

To quote from out State website, "This statement holds many truths. Michigan is a land of great splendors. Full of natural beauty, historical importance and citizens full of hope and energy as we enter into a new millennium. Michigan is also a place of economic opportunities."

This speaks to everything that is in the recipe for success:

- Seek beauty and joy
- Dream Big
- Leverage a talented and motivated team
- Learn from the past and have faith in the future
- Look about you!

What You Are Not Going to Do

"The ability to simplify means to eliminate the unnecessary so that the necessary may speak." – Hans Hofmann

---

One of the things you will quickly learn as your productivity leads to inevitable notoriety is that the more you do, the more people will ask you to do.

Exceed your targets at work and there will be new, higher targets. Do a great job on one board, and people will want you on a dozen boards.

Kaizen, the Japanese word for continuous improvement, is something toward which we should all strive. But be sure you understand your own personal definition of improvement. It does not necessarily mean doing more.

If you have had a business course, you likely know the name Peter Drucker. As the Father of Modern Management, Drucker gave us a number of good maxims including the concept of the "knowledge worker." What is not as well known, is that his advice for personal growth includes practicing "systematic abandonment."

He wrote, "People are effective because they say no...because they say, 'This isn't for me.'" He advocated regular reflection on what you can cut out of your daily routine to make room for something more rewarding.

I used to start every budget season by telling my team, "The time we invest in the new year will be just as important as the money we invest. Our success may well be determined by what we decide we are not going to do."

When was the last time you took out a pad of paper (or your iPad) and listed everything that takes up your time? Try keeping an activity log for 30 days and you will be surprised how much unproductive, unfulfilling things pop up on that list.

Then go back to that bucket list you have been keeping. You know, those things you have always wanted to do, but never had the time to do.

Start crossing things off of your activity list that are sucking energy or are not generating enough joy and enthusiasm for you. Replace them with things that are on your bucket list.

This will not be an easy exercise. Most self actualized people overbook themselves with things that are worthwhile and rewarding. You may decide you will want to stop doing something you enjoy to do something you enjoy more.

Understand, too, that stopping an activity will sometimes cause discomfort for people you care about. As you prepare for that tough conversation, remember Herb Swope's advice: "I cannot give you the formula for success, but I can give you the formula for failure, which is: Try to please everybody."

High performance people see the world as a huge orchard with hundreds of ripe apples falling off of every tree. They stand at the edge with a small basket made up of time and energy and want to try to grab every last every last apple, to make the most of every opportunity.

Some people are even paralyzed by the fear that they might pick the wrong apple and regret it. They are afraid to invest time in a new career path, a self development course, or a new relationship, end up not liking it, and wishing that they could have done something else.

Rather than taking any chance, they do nothing.

Your assignment: Live a life of ongoing self discovery.

As Drucker says, "What matters is that the knowledge worker, by the time he or she reaches middle age, has developed and nourished a human being rather than a tax accountant or a hydraulic engineer."

Realize that you do not have to do it all, that you can start down a road and decide to take a different road later on. Life really is that abundant apple orchard, but you do not have to eat every last one.

Nourish the exceptional human being that you are, and remember that, in the end, the only one you really have to make happy is you.

Cause and Effect

"We can evade reality, but we cannot evade the consequences of evading reality." – Ayn Rand

Let's talk about one of the most important laws of success. It's a fundamental, universal law that every spectacular achiever understands and practices every day. It's a law that influences everyone from the most destitute homeless person, to the multi-millionaire. If you understand and act based on this simple law, you will be successful, probably more successful than you may have ever imagined.

It is the law of cause and effect. Many of us know firsthand what it is like to touch a hot stove. My own hot stove story happened when I about ten years old. I methodically emptied the gunpowder out of a model rocket engine into a mound on my driveway to see what might happen if I put a match to it. It took about three weeks before my left hand recovered from the fiery flash that singed my skin, but I became intimately acquainted with the effect burning gunpowder has on the human hand when you cause it to ignite.

This same law, that scientists use to explain everything from the big bang to gravity, is critically important to our success and happiness as persons. When we use it in connection with positive, goal seeking behavior it will usually generate positive, productive results. By the same token, persons who use it with negative, tension relieving behavior will nearly always get negative results.

Here is another fact. You are already using the law of cause and effect every day, whether you know it or not. Take this test:

If you are in the sales profession, you know that the number of sales you make is in direct ratio to the number of sales presentations you make. And the number of sales presentations made is in direct ratio to the amount of prospecting you do.

So, if you're in the sales business, look at your past week on the job. How many sales did you make? How many sales presentations did you make? How much of your time was spent prospecting for qualified potential customers?

Whether you made one sale, ten sales or a hundred sales, your results are the fruits of your behaviors, the effects of your causes.

In the world of human achievement behaviors are our causes. How we behave every hour of every day is the cause that generates results or effects. The great sales guru Tom Hopkins likes to remind us that "We must do the most productive thing possible at every given moment." Earl Nightingale's magic formula for wealth is, "Our rewards in life are in direct proportion to our service." My own version of this wonderful old maxim is, "We are rewarded based on the value we add to the lives of others."

Now what do all of these ideas have in common? They are tied to our old friend cause and effect. If we do the most productive thing possible at every given moment, we will most certainly produce excellent results. The cause (productive behavior) generates the effect (excellent results). If we offer our clients the highest possible level of service we will retain those clients over the long haul and benefit from referral business. Outstanding service generates client retention and business growth. Cause and effect.

Look at your own personal behavior. If you are not happy with your current effects, you have only to change your causes (your behavior) and the results will change, often dramatically. My wife spent many years in search of some magic video tape or book that would help her lose weight. Our library is filled with diet books and exercise videos, but it was not until she made fundamental changes in her daily behavior that the pounds started to magically melt away.

Today she spends three mornings a week working out at the YMCA, is an active ballroom dancer and has transformed our diet from fatty fast foods to more nutritious fare. Friends constantly ask her for her success formula. She tells them that the formula is simple, but changing long standing behavior is hard. When she decided to initiate a new set of behaviors, the law of cause and effect kicked in and after 20 years of searching, she was behaving her way to her fitness objectives within six months.

David Crosby of the famous rock super group Crosby Stills and Nash is another example of the inexorable law of cause and effect. He writes in his autobiography, Long Time Gone, that from the moment he first tasted fame, he immersed himself in the popular drug laced lifestyle common among rock stars of the late sixties. He became addicted and spent the next two decades engaging in behaviors that landed him in jail and caused him to need a liver transplant to survive. David Crosby ultimately made a commitment to a different set of behaviors and was able to recover his life and return to performing. But others like Jim Morrison, Jimi Hendrix, Mama Cass, and Elvis are examples of how unhealthy causes generate equally unhealthy effects.

Think about how the law is impacting every corner of your life. Whether you like it or not, your current financial position, your fitness level, your personal and professional relationships are all the results or effects of your behavioral causes.

So how do we enter the rarified world of those who seem to have the Midas touch? What can we do to enrich our interaction with our co workers and loved ones? How can we increase our energy, our productivity, our results and our income?

The best way to use the law of cause and effect to our benefit is to model the behavior of people that already have achieved the results we desire. Make it your business to study the habits of the people in your line of work who seem to always be leading the field. How do they spend their days, who do they associate with, what education and training to they have, what do they read, how do they dress and speak, what do they do with their spare time. Become intimately familiar with the behaviors and routines of the people you admire. How do men and women with strong and happy relationships interact with one another? What is the daily fitness and diet program recommended by people who coach Olympic athletes? Once you begin to understand and model the behaviors of the people who already are achieving the goals you desire, it is only a matter of time until you experience the same results.

Now we can spend years studying the lives of successful people, but we will not come one step closer to joining their ranks unless we make the decision to irrevocably change our behaviors. This is called: Commitment. It is the key ingredient to every goal that has ever been reached. It is the corner stone of every skyscraper every built, and burns like a fire in the hearts of every football team that has ever been to the super bowl. So I will say it again. We will not come one step closer to achieving any of our dreams until we make a commitment to change our behavior.

If you find yourself mired in longstanding unproductive, tension relieving behaviors, reinventing yourself might seem like an insurmountable task. So here is the secret to making a commitment to change your life for the better: Attack each challenge one day at a time.

When he was eight years old Glenn Cunningham was severely burned in a gasoline explosion. Doctors were unanimous in telling the young Kansas boy that he would never walk again. But Glenn Cunningham had goals and commitment. He understood the law of cause and effect and attacked his goals one day at a time. He not only learned to walk, but became one of the premiere runners of the 1930s, competing in the 1932 Olympics and becoming the worlds fastest miler in 1938. Cunningham went on to earn a Doctorate at New York University and developed physical training systems for the Navy that are still used today.

Now we may not face a serious physical challenge like Glenn Cunningham, but we can benefit from his one-day-at-a-time success formula. As the old Chinese proverb says, "A journey of a thousand miles begins with a single step." Your first step is to create a personal business plan.

Your personal business plan should address every corner of your life and it involves writing down a set of personal goals.

The art of goal setting is something we will cover in detail later on.

There is a useful acrostic to help you with this process. When you set goals, make sure that they are SMART goals. The S in SMART stands for Specific. The more detail you give to your goal, the more likely you will be able to reach it. M stands for Measurable. You will never achieve an objective without knowing what constitutes its completion. The A and R in our acrostic stand for Achievable and Realistic. Your goals should stretch you, but should always be within your reach. Setting a goal to climb Mount Everest beginning a week from Saturday is achievable for the trained mountaineer who is already in Nepal, and in possession of the tools and the team needed to help her reach the summit, but I am sure that you will agree that it is a stretch to set such a goal if you have never climbed anything higher than the stairs to your bedroom. If you decide to set an audacious goal that involves achieving a number of interim goals along the way, give yourself the Time to achieve it. That's what the T in SMART stands for: Timely. Give every goal a deadline for completion. Set mid-course correction points where you can adjust your game plan to take advantage of what you have learned in pursuit of your goal and, take time to celebrate your progress.

Write your goals down on a piece of paper. Put them in your Palm Pilot or paste them to your bathroom mirror with a post-it note. Always keep your goals in the front of your mind, to take advantage of the human brain's miraculous subconscious goal-seeking mechanism. We become what we think about.

Set goals that are SMART:
- Specific
- Measurable

155

- Achievable
- Realistic
- Timely

Set goals for your career, your physical health, your intellectual and spiritual growth, your family and personal relationships. Studies show us that the people who are in the process of achieving meaningful goals across every corner of their being tend to be consistently happier, healthier, enjoy a better night's sleep and have a wide array of enriching, satisfying relationships.

Do it today. Revisit your own personal formula for success. Create a personal business plan. Study people you know who have already achieved the success you desire. Carefully and consistently model their behaviors, and in no time at all, you will be on the road to reaching your dreams, achieving your goals, and living the life you were born to live.

It is the law of cause and effect and it can work for you.

How to Become Rich

"To me, money is a means to do good. I reached a point in my life
where I had enjoyed tremendous business success
that afforded my family everything we could possibly want.
My wife and I then decided that we could use our wealth
to make a difference. So we created the
Broad Foundations to do four things:
to improve urban public education,
to support innovative scientific and medical research,
to foster art appreciation for audiences worldwide
and to support civic initiatives in Los Angeles." – Ely Broad

Back in the days when I was nearing graduation from College, I was filled with idealism and energy. Even though I had worked my way through school at a local radio station, I was still relatively clueless about the big, shining world that waited for me at the other end of my graduation walk.

One of my professors invited an honest to goodness TV salesman into our class that senior spring, and after he imparted wisdom that I have long since forgotten, I found myself among a handful of students who cornered him afterwards to ask him for the "Secret of Success."

When I posed the question, he rubbed his nose in deep thought and said, "Know what you want and don't stop till you get it."

Several years ago, I had the opportunity to speak to a group of about 50 college seniors attending the Michigan Association of Broadcasters Convention in Lansing. Afterward I found myself

157

cornered by a couple of students. I anticipated being consulted for my great wisdom and was a little taken aback when they thrust a package of paper into my hands.

"Here is my resume," said one, "Can you help me find a job?"

"What's your goal?" I asked.

The question seemed to stop them short for a moment. Then one said, "To get a TV production job."

The other said, "I want to be rich."

"Let's start with your dream," I said to the second student, "What would you do if you could work for love instead of for money?"

When I evaluated the blank stares I got in return, I was reminded again of the late-great Earl Nightingale's maxim on why it is so easy to earn more money, have more of the things we want and achieve just about any objective we set our minds to.

The reason more men and women do not make it to that top percentile of the most successful people in our society is that so few, so very few, spend any constructive time thinking about how to do it.

The road to real success in life has so few people running the race that everyone can be a winner.

So let's talk about how to become rich. I believe the secret is hidden in the four P's. They are my sure-fire, easy-to-remember formula for achieving any goal you set in your life. They work in every situation for every human being regardless of your background, parents, financial status, talent or education.

Here they are:
- PASSION
- PLANNING
- PERSEVERANCE
- PERPETUATION

To be successful in any endeavor you must first discover what really turns you on, you need to develop a road map on how to get where you want to go, you have to stick with the program no matter what, and once you achieve your dream you need to help pass it on to others.

Now that you've heard the four P's, let's dig into what they really mean.

Here's number one: Before you can be successful, you must seek your PASSION.

What really excites you? If you could take a pill that would guarantee that you would succeed in anything you tried, what would you do? Think about the values that are important to you. A wise person once said that inner peace only happens when activities and values match.

Passion is what separates Julia Roberts, Harrison Ford, Norah Jones and Billy Joel from the millions of us who sing in the shower and dream of a movie career. Passion is what kept Bret Farve and Cal Ripkin, Jr. coming back to the game on the days when their knees and muscles were screaming for a day off. Passion is what helped Viktor Frankl and thousands of others survive the horrors of the concentration camps. Passion kept

Thomas Edison on task when he failed over 150 times in his quest to create electric light.

Taking time to explore what activities, people, places and things really excite you can help guarantee that you will select the right job, the right home, and the right life partner.

Finding your passion requires disciplined process of THINKING. Now if thinking were an animal, today it would be on the endangered species list. My two college student friends probably spend more time planning a vacation then they do thinking about their personal goals and objectives.

So THINK. Think regularly and with a purpose. Think with a pencil and a pad of paper close at hand. Think at the same time every day. When you develop the habit of thinking, you will be surprised at how many great ideas seem to fly out of your mind and onto the paper.

Once you understand your passion, you need a PLAN.

David Jensen of UCLA discovered that people with goals earn more than twice as much money as people without goals. They are also happier, healthier and have better relationships with friends and loved ones. There is no doubt about it, goals are good for you.

Review our discussion of SMART goals in the chapter titled "Cause and Effect" and make a note of these additional bullet points:

- For each goal you set, identify, "What's in it for me?" You will be able to stick with your plan if you are fully aware of the benefits.
- Set a variety of goals: big goals, small goals, short range goals, long range goals.

- Set goals for mind, body and spirit. Zig Ziglar is the king of goal setting training. He believes in a goal wheel with spokes radiating out in each of seven segments of your life:
- Physical
- Mental
- Financial
- Career
- Family
- Personal
- Spiritual
- Don't set more than four goals for a particular day.
- Break down your big goals into bite size smaller goals to ensure that they are attainable.
- Anticipate the obstacles you may encounter on your way to your goals.
- List the people, skills, organizations and resources, you will need to develop to achieve your goals.

Again, set a deadline for when you will achieve your goals. Having a deadline helps to focus your activities.

Once you have a passionate objective and a detailed plan about how to get there, there are two important facts you need to know.

Number one: You will fail along the road to success.

Remember always that failure is only an event, not a person. Henry Ford started three different Ford Motor Companies before founding the organization we now associate with his name. Domino's Pizza founder Tom Monaghan says that he made so many mistakes along the way that he often thought about giving up his dream. When my friend Mike Dyer and I were starting out in real estate, we lived by Tommy Hopkins' wise words, "Never see failure as failure, but only as a learning experience."

The second thing to remember is the one word that can guarantee your success.

And the word is: Attitude.

As the great American Psychologist and Philosopher William James says, "Your ATTITUDE will be the single biggest factor in determining the extent of your success."

Think about the leaders you admire. It's a good bet that they all share a positive outlook on life. They expect good things to happen and on the occasions when clouds cross the horizon, they seem to have infinite reservoirs of resiliency and bounce back from failure to success again and again.

Armed with the knowledge that failures are the stepping stones to success, you can develop a positive attitude that will help you PERSEVERE to reach your dreams.

Calvin Coolidge is credited with this classic quote, "Nothing in the world can take the place of persistence. Talent will not; nothing is more common than unsuccessful men with talent. Genius will not; unrewarded genius is almost a proverb. Education will not; the world is full of educated derelicts. Persistence and determination are omnipotent."

Perseverance means continually testing new ideas, seeking feedback and discarding what does not work. When I started up the World Beacon international radio network, we spent over $20,000.00 on broadcasting equipment. After continual experimentation we ended up feeding our transmitters around the world with a $2000.00 dollar computer and free, open-source MP3 software. My Emergency Email Network went through four different vendors in search of the perfect email solution. Based on what we learned, we ended up writing it ourselves and patenting the new process.

Here is a skill that can help you persevere; whether your goal is to become an elite athlete, a musician, doctor, a minister or a business person, imagine now how that person behaves and start now to act as would the person that has already achieved your goal. How do they dress, how do they speak, what education do they have, what do they read, how do they spend their days. Demonstrate these behaviors everyday in the unfailing kindness you show towards others, the discipline with which you follow your plan, and the integrity and character you radiate out into the world around you. Begin now to act like the person you hope to be and you will become that person.

A successful life is all about cause and effect. My favorite quote from Earl Nightingale is this, "Our rewards in life will always be in direct proportion to our service." Or as it says in the Bible, "As ye sow, so shall ye reap."

With passion, plan and perseverance you will overcome every obstacle and in time you will achieve every meaningful goal you set. Others will call you lucky, but there is really no luck involved. You are just taking advantage of the law of cause and effect. Your causes are excellent and your effects are equally as good.

And finally, what do you do when you become what others call successful? The last P in our formula is PERPETUATION.

When you become successful, you will want to pass it on to others.

163

Ely and Edith Broad are classic examples of people who are working to perpetuate their success in the community. The Broads have been immensely successful by adding value in the business world. And now they spend a good portion of their time serving on non-profit boards, investing in things they are passionate about.

During the Depression, steel baron Andrew Carnegie built hundreds of libraries across the nation so that people could have access to the knowledge that could lead them to achieve their goals.

Drive across the Michigan State University campus and you'll see dozens of buildings named for the wonderful men and women who continue to perpetuate their legacy of success through their generous contributions to the Institution.

Share your abundance, be a mentor and inspire others to excellence. Always give more than you get.

The American mystic Ram Dass says that a funny thing about reaching a major goal is that it often seems to be less and less important the closer we get to it. In elementary school we dreamed of reaching middle school, but after we graduate from high school, that same fifth grade class seems small and insignificant.

In the end, your definition of success might mirror the words of Ralph Waldo Emerson:

> *To laugh often and much;*
> *to win the respect of intelligent people*
> *and the affection of children;*
> *to earn the appreciation of honest critics*
> *and endure the betrayal of false friends;*

to appreciate beauty;
to find the best in others; to leave the world a bit better,
whether by a healthy child, a garden,
or a redeemed social condition;
to know even one life has breathed easier because you have lived.
This is to have succeeded.

The more goals you achieve, the more you learn that Success is a process, not an event.

There is a great book called Flow written by a scholar named Mihaly Csikszentmihalyi. He talks about the feeling you get when you are in the midst of working on a difficult problem and begin to make progress. The exhilaration, the energy and the excitement of pursuing a worthy goal is his definition of Flow. Successful people say that this "in the zone" feeling of pleasure, concentration and achievement is what it is all about.

The process of seeking your passion, building a game plan, overcoming the obstacles through healthy relationships and continuing education, and perpetuating the dream by sharing these secrets with others. That's the true definition of richness.

PASSION

PLANNING

PERSEVERANCE

PERPETUATION

Now you know it. Go out and do it.

165

All Glory is Fleeting

"It is not titles that honor men, but men that honor titles."
– Niccolo Machiavelli

We pay a lot of money to those who are willing to walk closest to the cliff not because we're proud of their courage, but because they might fall off of it.

Our thirst for novelty drives athletes to steroids and tempts those hungry for notoriety to seek short cuts.

But in the end, few things endure in our world. Todays stars populate tomorrows reality shows. And fame has a way of making all but a few, self destruct.

There are a thousand arguments for humility. Here are two of my favorites.

"For over a thousand years Roman conquerors returning from the wars enjoyed the honor of a triumph, a tumultuous parade. In the procession came trumpeters, musicians and strange animals from conquered territories, together with carts laden with treasure and captured armaments. The conqueror rode in a triumphal chariot, the dazed prisoners walking in chains before him. Sometimes his children robed in white stood with him in the chariot or rode the trace horses. A slave stood behind the conqueror holding a golden crown and whispering in his ear a warning: that all glory is fleeting." – Gen. George S. Patton, Jr.

And this:

Former Secretary of State James Baker notes, "Someone asked me what was the most important thing I had learned since being in Washington. I replied that it was the fact that temporal power is fleeting." Baker remembers driving through the White House gates and noticing a man walking alone on Pennsylvania Avenue. The man was the Secretary of State in a previous administration. "There he was alone – no reporters, no security, no adoring public, no trappings of power. Just one solitary man alone with his thoughts. And that mental picture continually serves to remind me of the impermanence of power and the impermanence of place."

The Coach

*"People will degrade your success and amplify your failures.
Pursue success anyway."*

Colleen and I were still savoring the victory. We were among 78,000 witnesses who saw MSU Football Coach Mark Dantonio make the gutsiest call of his Spartan career. Rather than press his young kicker for a 47 yard overtime field goal... and a tie, he called for "The Little Giant".. and went for the win.

Holder Aaron Bates had been a high school quarterback. Receiver Charlie Gantt is a senior with the desire all Spartans share: to make a lasting mark in the program. Together they choreographed a pass pattern that found Gantt open in the Northeast corner of the Irish end zone.

"The Little Giant" worked. Game over.

Just hours later I got the call. Coach Dantonio was at Sparrow Hospital. He had suffered a heart attack.

At 1PM on Sunday afternoon, I was with about 20 reporters, listening to Dr. Chris D'Haem talk about the procedure that saved our Coach's life. Athletic Director Mark Hollis said that things like this pull Spartans together. And interim Head Coach Don Treadwell, a gifted teacher who will someday own a similar title permanently, vowed that Dantonio's system would continue and the team would persevere.

Throughout the press conference, all I could think about was the inexorable pressure that a person takes on when he or she takes on the mantle of leadership and becomes a coach.

We expect coaches to be infallible and superhuman. We expect them to make the right decisions every time. We expect them to say the right thing, attract the best talent and control their team's behavior, on and off the field.

And we expect them to win.

College coaches carry an added burden. The press for an elite program often requires taking a chance on young motor geniuses who struggle academically and socially. Student athletes must maintain their grades and their physical performance in an environment where academics and athletics constantly contend. Peer pressure and the allure of fame is an ever present distraction and the white hot spotlight of notoriety puts every kid's stumble on the front page.

When anything goes wrong, we blame the coach. Yet coaches endure. Sometimes they win, sometimes they lose. Always they can make a life-changing difference.

And so it is with life.

People will degrade your success and amplify your failures. Pursue success anyway.

Our world demands instant and continuous success. Build slowly, carefully and well. Build a career and a life that will last.

Others expect infallibility. Nobody is perfect so don't be afraid to fail.. and learn from it.

169

For many, winning is the only thing. Have compassion for the victor and the vanquished. You will eventually know them both, personally.

We tend to define success as a scoreboard of material acquisition. True happiness is found in fulfilling relationships and doing good things.

Take care of your body. Nothing else matters if your marvelous machine doesn't work.

And always remember that the best legacy we can leave is to teach others what a successful life is really all about. You may be criticized and second guessed. Small minds may blame you for their own shortcomings. There will be days when it feels like you aren't making progress.

But you are.

Model the behavior. Teach.

Be a coach.

Do What You Can

"Do what you can, with what you have, where you are."
– Theodore Roosevelt

Every community has it's own Secret CEO Society, that small percentage of people who seem to do all the work.

These are the innovators, the idea generators, the ones who volunteer to lead even when the job might not be fun and no other hands go up. They have known pain, sometimes a lot of it, but they haven't lost their love for life, their curiosity, their resiliency, or their sense of humor. They tend to invest more in philanthropic interests and less in material things for themselves. They have egos, but they are exponentially smaller than the causes they choose to support. They are almost always lending a hand, cooking you a meal, giving you a ride, or asking you lots of questions about the things that interest you.

In every town where Colleen and I have lived, I've sought out the Secret CEO Society. There is no national organization, and although they may see each other at weekly service club luncheons and serve on a lot of the same boards, they rarely get together to talk about their own hopes and dreams.

That's why I try to find them and bring them together.

It's usually very early in the morning. Secret CEOs are busy people. And our conversation surrounds two questions:

How can we help you?

171

How can we make this a better place to live?

In Albuquerque, one of our Secret CEOs shared how he dramatically cut his company's health care premiums, by hiring a Physician's Assistant to directly serve his employees. This PA was on site every day. She was the first stop before his team went to their family docs, offered free sports physical exams for all employee kids and promoted general healthy living. This culture of wellness generated an economic benefit for the company's bottom line. But at least one person saw it differently, the woman who's life was saved when the PA discovered a lump that turned out to be cancer in a very early and treatable stage.

I was in awe of this Secret CEO and asked him what made him think to provide this unique benefit.

"I do what I can," he said.

Compare this to my Friend, Elizabeth Battiste. She doesn't consider herself a CEO. She's a junior at MSU.

Somewhere in her 20 years of life, despite a number of pretty substantial obstacles, she decided to be a leader. In addition to being a full time student, she is President of the MSU Sexual Assault Crisis Intervention Team, has internships at the Community Relations Coalition and at MSU Student Services, has served as a legislative aide and a peer educator. She is a role model for everyone around her and always seems to be finding some way to add value wherever she goes. She does this all without a car and without the traditional family support systems many of us had to rely on during our college years.

The other night, I asked her how she can accomplish so much She smiled and said, "I do what I can."

When I meet these people I always think of one of my favorite quotes.

"I am only one, but still I am one. I cannot do everything, but still I can do something. And because I cannot do everything I will not refuse to do the something that I can do."

Powerful and profound, even before you learn that Helen Keller said it.

Here's your challenge: Think of another small way you can engage to "do what you can".

Tolerance

The last pre-game event I visited during the 2010 regular football season was Sparty's Middle Eastern Tailgate. It was a co-production of the MSU Jewish Student Union and the MSU Arab Cultural Society. The food was terrific. But that wasn't the miracle.

What I saw were Arabs and Jews hugging one another, interacting and working on ways that they can improve the larger community together.

It blew me away.

If these kids can figure out how to coexist and perhaps even love each another, why can't the rest of the world do it?

We all chafe at the new TSA procedures that require us to walk, virtually naked, through bomb detectors. If we decline, TSA employees in rubber gloves get to grope us. This degradation is supposedly for our safety, because a small number of people who hate us can't get along.

There is no doubt that the world is rife with complicated problems.

There are still knuckleheads in this country who think that people who don't look like they do don't deserve to be equals. Generations of killing begets generations of revenge as two cultures fight over a strip of Middle Eastern land 146 square

174

miles in size. Thousands of people who don't see a productive future will turn their bodies into bombs, rather than reach for their dreams.

Heck, watch any of the vitriolic, misleading and downright cruel political ads that aired during the most recent election cycle from the perspective of an alien. You'll conclude that our two parties have evolved into machines that exist to destroy one another.

It's easy to retreat into negativity. Demagogues feed on fear, uncertainty and and distrust. It's much easier to tear someone down than it is to build someone up. Tyrants rise amid hopelessness. Bad news sells newspapers. And on TV, priority is often given to violence. To quote a news director friend, "If it bleeds it leads".

What can we do to move this global hate-fest away from self destruction?

It can only happen one person at a time. And -you- have to model the behavior.

If you are what others consider successful, seek ways to bring the least of them along with you.

If you have abundant resources, become a philanthropist.

If you happen to identify with a particular race, religion or ethnicity, make it your life's work to interact with and understand those who are different. If you do, it will encourage them to try to better understand you.

If you are taught that someone else's politics or sexual preference is bad, open a bible to Genesis 1:27 and realize that

God created ALL of us in His image. And you might do well to read Matthew 5:44, where Jesus said, "Love your enemies and pray for those who persecute you".

Don't let political correctness stop you from being who you are. Speak out but be sensitive. Be aware that what you say and how you say it can be discomforting and hurtful to others.

Protect those you love from harm, but never intentionally injure someone else.

Seek to understand the things that hold people back from becoming the best that they can be. Be a catalyst to remove barriers and provide the tools to help others envision their dreams and become their best.

Don't give in to fear. If you do, the bad guys win. As Susan Jeffers writes, "Feel the fear, and do it anyway."

Act peacefully. Dr. King and Mahatma Gandhi moved mountains with non-violent force.

And be patient. This pain we all feel has deep roots. Change takes time. It may not happen in your lifetime, but you can push the flywheel. Time and again, history shows us that one person CAN transform the world. Others are watching. If your motives are genuine, they will join you.

And even if they don't, consider tolerance. Acknowledging our differences is the first step toward understanding.

When more people see a hopeful future, fewer people will be attracted to the unhappy minority who would destroy it.

I recently had the honor of chartering the MSU Latino Alumni Interest Group. I told them, "Tenemos sólo una raza. La Raza Humana." We come from many places but in the end we are all part of only one race: The Human Race.

If we can discover and debate from a place of diversity, there is a much better chance that we will make the right decisions when we act as one.

Keep all of this in mind as you go about your daily activities this week. Seek to understand. Model the behavior.

And watch what happens.

Winning

When my Spartans played Purdue in the second to last game of the storybook 2010 football season, they almost stopped my heart. We played inconsistently for three quarters and got behind a team we should have dominated. It wasn't until the last minute that our come-from-behind victory was assured.

I Tweeted, "Ugly, but got the 'W'." to my friends.

My friend, MSU Athletic Director Mark Hollis, instantly tweeted back, "There is no such thing as an ugly win."

There is.

Ben Lichtenwalner rails against the toxic leadership that so-called winners all to often inject into our organizations. In his Servant Leadership Manifesto, he writes, "You see it in business, when narcissistic executives build golden parachutes and steal from tomorrow to make today look good. You see it in Academia when professors forget the students in their march toward self-promotion and prominence in their field. You see it in churches where the minister's name appears above the savior's. You see it in charities that put growth and recognition ahead of the needs of the suffering. You see it in government when politicians promote themselves over the needs of their constituents."

Yes, it is possible to win ugly, but that is not what real winning is all about.

Winners play by the rules: History is littered with those who have bent and broken the rules to get to the top. In time, everybody who twists the truth get's caught and the ages will record your true intentions. Play fair, win fair.

Winners give their best effort: The easy prize is hollow. And you do not have to finish first to be a winner. Vince Lombardi said, "Winning isn't everything, but the will to win is everything."

Winners learn from their mistakes: All winners have failed. Many have failed often. A mistake can be a powerful teacher. To paraphrase Denis Waitley, "Losers live in the past. Winners learn from the past, focus on the present and plan for the future."

Winners are flexible: The world is constantly changing. Winners change with it and are often change agents. I love this Maria Robinson chestnut, "Nobody can go back and start a new beginning, but anyone can start today and make a new ending."

Winners plan ahead: They are always imagining the challenges and opportunities of tomorrow and prepare for them today. As the old saying goes, it pays to plan ahead. It was not raining when Noah built the ark.

Winners never give up: Jim Cash wrote screenplays for 15 years before he hit a home run with "Top Gun". Tom Monaghan admits he did "everything wrong" on his way to creating Domino's Pizza. Henry Ford went broke five times before creating the Ford Motor Company that we know today.

Winners are humble: Most successful people are also nice people. They may achieve great things, but they never forget the hard work, the luck, and those who helped them get there.

Winners make more winners: This is, perhaps, the greatest trait of a true winner. They recognize that they can't do it alone and inspire others to greatness, leaving other true winners in their wake.

Life is hard. It requires constant commitment, patience, tenacity and resiliency. And the irony is this: There is just as much pain, inconvenience and effort in an unfulfilled life as there is in an exceptional life.

It is your choice. Choose to win.

Hope

The holiday parties I attended this year seemed to have a common theme. I inevitably ran into people who think there is a lack of opportunity out there these days. Many are feeling stuck in assignments that don't tap their full potential, or are afraid that their comfortable existence might be disrupted at any moment.

The news tells us that our economy is still weak. The threat of a double-dip recession is out there. Between technology and cheap off shore labor, it sometimes feels like the American Dream is dying.

This isn't new. Every generation faces it's test. And there is always opportunity out there for those willing to grab the brass ring.

One of the best dimensions of my life is that I run into people every day who are doing great things and having great fun. Some say that if achievement were easy, everybody would be a star. But the reality is that just anyone can take steps right now toward a more happy, productive and hopeful adventure.

Life is fired at us point blank. The old saying that we can't choose what happens to us, but we can choose how we react has never been more true.

How can we be more like those wonderful people who seem to thrive, even in the most trying times? How can we keep the faith and tap our "capacity for hope" in a world that often seems hopeless?

Empty your emotional wheelbarrow – We all push an invisible wheelbarrow around that we fill up with all the emotion we must stifle to survive the tough times. If we let it get too full, we can't push it anymore and our bodies will react in dangerous ways. Find a safe place and blow out as much of your pent up anger and sadness as you can. This "clearing" is an exercise we all need to do with regularity to dump some of the load out of our wheelbarrow and give us the capacity to push harder and further.

Envision happiness – What does it look like and feel like? When you were at your happiest, what were you doing? What's stopping you from being happy right now? Resolve today to chase your happiness. Life is too short not to.

Design your ideal life – What is your definition of a life well lived? I'll give you a clue. It isn't sitting on the beach and sipping umbrella drinks all day. Who are the most fulfilled people you know? What do they do? How do they face a challenge? Write down every dimension of your Wonderful Life. Where willyou live? Where will you work? How will you spend your days? Paint the picture in high definition and full color, right down to the diet and exercise plan.

Take stock of your people portfolio - Time is the one finite resource that we all share. How are you spending yours? Who are the people who can help you get to where you want to be? Are there energy suckers in your orbit that you need to de-prioritize to make room for more enriching relationships? Do you have enough quality time in your day set aside to nurture those who are most important to you?

Create a step by step action plan – When you have a clear definition of happiness and have painted a vivid picture of your ideal life, building the stepping stones to get there can be quickly done. It won't be easy. Pieces of your uncomfortable current reality will creep into the picture. Identify those unproductive patterns. Be brutally honest with yourself about your motives for everything you do. Create clear, reasonable and achievable goals. And write them down.

Begin – The hardest step is first step, followed by the personal commitment to continue. Research tells us that it takes 30 days to turn a behavior into a habit. Even then it's easy to fall off course without tenacious resolve. As Ghandi wrote, "Keep your thoughts positive because your thoughts become your words. Keep your words positive because your words become your behavior. Keep your behavior positive because your behavior becomes your habits. Keep your habits positive because your habits become your values. Keep your values positive because your values become your destiny."

Be grateful – Everything that happens to us, even the worst things, can be stepping stones, if we learn from them. Make your heaviest burdens the defining moments of your existence. And be as grateful for every bump in the road as your are for every beautiful sunset. You need to experience one to fully appreciate the other.

Have hope -Christopher Reeve said, "Once you choose hope, anything's possible." And he said it after his riding accident robbed him of his superpowers. When the world says, "Give up," Hope whispers, "Try it one more time."

Having a capacity for hope when those around you have lost theirs can move you more quickly toward any goal. But the true magic of hope is that it's contagious. Hope's infectious nature can also inspire others to move beyond negativity and fear and into the sunlight of opportunity.

Clear. Envision. Design. Surround yourself with positive people. Plan. Begin. Be grateful.

And keep the faith!

In the Long Run

---

*"The Race is not always to the swift,
but to those who can keep running."*

Running has been an important meditation practice for much of my adult life. There is no high like a runner's high. When the endorphins are flowing, new ideas seem to flow with them. A regular commitment to cardiovascular activity has benefits that extend well beyond the physical body.

Time and circumstance derailed my passion for much of the last seven years. Returning to the place where I first laced up my Adidas inspired me to again attempt an every-other-day regimen.

I had forgotten how many things about running parallel the road to a successful life. Here are just a few:

Stretch yourself: This primary exercise that precedes every run makes it possible for you to put in more miles with less pain. Stretching outside of your comfort zone in life has the same effect.

Get out there and do it: As Woody Allen observed, "Ninety percent of life is just showing up." For me the hardest part of running is getting out of bed and walking out the front door. Once I am on the road, I am always glad I did it. Step beyond your self created obstacles and watch the magic happen.

Run with others: The thing that really got me back on track was RunKeeper.com. This nifty site ties in with an app on my

GPS enabled iPhone that tracks my mileage and route. The real motivator here is that I share my activities with a selected group of accountability buddies, other Run Keeper members who can see what I am doing. Character may well be defined as what happens when nobody else is watching, but it is hard to underestimate the power of having a friend watching over your shoulder.

You learn more from the races you lose than the races you win. Watch and learn from those who run in front of you.

Attack the hills: A great thought from an unknown philosopher: Nobody trips over mountains. It is the small pebble that causes you to stumble. Pass all the pebbles in your path and you will find you have crossed the mountain.

Enjoy the view: I like to run just before sunrise. In the Fall, Orion keeps me company in the South and the orange skies in the east remind me that every day is a new beginning. My per-mile times always suffer because, at some point, I have to stop and drink in this steadfast miracle.

Keep at it: Life is a marathon, not a sprint. The Japanese proverb, "Fall seven times, get up eight," is the true essence of life. There will always be obstacles and setbacks. The road is littered with good people who gave up too early while History celebrates great people who never gave up. Robert Brault had the right idea when he wrote, "Stubbornly persist, and you will find that the limits of your stubbornness go well beyond the stubbornness of your limits."

As the Buddhists might say, "If we are facing in the right direction, all we have to do is keep on running." If you have bracketed your passion and have goals that support it, get in

the race and you will be surprised how far you can go in the
long run.

Endurance

"Endurance is one of the most difficult disciplines, but it is to the one who endures that the final victory comes." - Buddha

Race day.

I look across the vastness of the participants who wait at the starting line and wonder. How will I perform? Will I embarrass myself? Can I finish? Is this all worth it?

The klaxon sounds and we are off.

The first mile is one of the easiest, and yet, also one of the hardest. The field is thick with competitors. Despite stretching, my muscles feel tight. The heart and lungs have not found their rhythm. I try to ignore it all and hold a breathless conversation with my race partner, Jo.

As we cross the second mile, everyone who is running the 5K peels off to the right. Jo and I choose the road less traveled, but I have an envious thought: Why did I decide to run the longer race? Our larger contingent of friends is taking the easier route and will be done with this much sooner.

Jo looks over her shoulder at mile three. I'm twenty feet behind now. "Are you okay," she asks? I've told her from the start to run her own race and not to wait up for me. It is a short ten weeks since I returned to the road and over a decade since I have competed. I smile, give her a thumbs up and point to the road ahead. The message: Go for it. I have your back.

At mile four the unaccustomed hills are taking their toll. My calves are on fire and it feels like everyone is passing me. My mind starts to rationalize the idea of walking for a bit, but my spirit will not have it. Follow what your coaches say. Maintain your stride and cadence. Stay focused. I turn up the music in my headphones.

Mile five is the worst. The hills seem endless. Even maintaining my stride, it feels like I am walking this. Everyone is passing me and my partner is well past the finish line. The advice to "forget the clock and enjoy this" does not resonate. I am a competitor and am angry that my fitness level is holding me back. I wish I were faster. I wish I hadn't agreed to do this. I wish I had started training much sooner. This is not fun.

At mile six, the finish line comes into sight. From somewhere deep within the adrenalin kicks in. I pound up the last hill and sprint. Where did this energy come from? The pain is gone. Blood carries the oxygenated fuel to my legs and they respond. The runners high that has been absent all morning rolls through every cell of my body like a warm ocean wave. I see the huge clock that is documenting this mediocre performance and decide that I will not let it spin past another minute before I cross the line. My entire body feels in sync. The remaining competitors vanish. I am totally focused. The wind blows the sweat back from my face and I can feel it jumping off the back of my neck like rain drops.

Crossing the finish line brings the same exhilaration, whether you are first or near the back of the pack. Yes, you finished slower than two thirds of the participants, but you showed up. There are hundreds of thousands of other people out there who won't even lace up running shoes, let alone do this. My mind begins to ponder the possibilities. With time and effort, my performance will improve. There will still be miles that are not fun, but there will be many more miles that are. The running community is like no other. I have many new instant friends. And the side benefits of the exercise far outweigh the inconvenience.

If this were easy, it would not be worth the work. There is joy that mixes with the pain. Knowing one helps you appreciate the importance of the other.

This is why I run. This is why we live.

Jo comes down the hill with two bottles of water. We embrace as only soul mates can.

The Father Factor

"Make a difference for all the world."

My father is The "Real" Scott Westerman. I am the third in a line that started with his dad back in 1895. I have always felt richly blessed to have been born into a family with the father and mother I was dealt. On Father's Day in my dad's 85th year, I sat down to ask him what lessons he learned from his father. I present them here, not necessarily as recommendations, but solely for your consideration.

Make a difference for all the world: Grandpa was a distinguished music major at the University of Michigan, turned Methodist Missionary, turned distinguished Ohio pastor, turned electronics enthusiast. He and Grandma worked the mission field in the darkest corners of the Bolivian Andes. As pastor of Grace Methodist Church in Dayton, he built an army of choirs totaling over 200 of the congregation's 1400 members. He offered free voice lessons to every choir member who wanted them. I have a box of his sermons in my closet, each one succeeding in translating the often confusing chapter and verse into meaningful messages that inspired his parishioners to model the Golden Rule.

Give your all: Dad admits that he learned much from his father from a distance. Grandpa was always working. Both Dad and I have comforting memories of seeing the reflections of the car lights dancing across our bedroom walls late in the evening when our respective fathers came home. Grandpa's dedication sometimes surpassed his physical stamina. One terrifying memory Dad has was a Sunday when the pastor did not show up at church at the appointed time. When calls to the house went unanswered they rushed home to find him sleeping so deeply that he did not hear the phone, or respond to the loud pounding on the front door. It took two weeks for him to recover, but he was soon back at it.

Seek balance: Dad believes that it was the work load and not Grandpa's milieu of childhood health issues that brought on his first heart attack, at age 45. To be sure, it did not ultimately stop him from grabbing life by the mane. He would have three more attacks before finally succumbing in his 80s.

Be inclusive: Both my father, and my own personal commitment to diversity have roots in Grandpa's courageous integration of the church Boy Scout troop, long before it was the common thing to do. And Grandpa and Grandma had a habit of adopting church members with disabilities and going the extra mile to help each get the most out of life.

Develop diverse interests: Grandpa was a musician, vocalist, a basketball, track, gymnastics, swimming and boxing enthusiast. In addition to his passion for fishing, he was a bird watcher, gardener and dog lover. Late in life, he developed an interest in electronics, building antennas for his shortwave receiver and recording television and radio programming for soldiers serving in Viet Nam.

Have faith: Grandpa's was a Christian life, but like the Dali Lama, my own father would encourage you to seek your own spiritual path. Faith, whether it be in deity or the ordered mysteries of science is at once alluring and baffling, exuberant and frustrating. If you build your own foundation of faith it can keep you grounded through the strongest hurricanes, the harshest spotlight and the darkest night.

Be well read: Being up on current events and the latest literature was part of all our lives growing up. The things we discovered in newspapers and between the covers of good books danced through our minds, leaving notions that often sprouted like seeds into new and even more powerful ideas.

Get an education and seek to become a better person: Most of us are but a generation or two away from a time when college was the exception to the rule. In our parents and grandparents time, education meant drinking knowledge with a desert thirst, trying to fully understand and sometimes challenge what we were taught. Good grades a goal but were secondary to the desire for real comprehension. Those learning skills served our forefathers well as we recovered from the Great Depression, fought a World War and learned to make sense of things like the Iron Curtain. Having the courage to face any personal demons you may have will also teach your children that we are all imperfect, it is okay to recognize it, and that life is too short not to get help while you enjoy the ride.

Don't do it all yourself: Both my grandfather and my dad were the first ones to admit that they could not have been effective parents without help. In our home, my mom was well prepared and totally dedicated to providing that help. But it went well beyond their union. They made sure that when we needed them, the right teachers appeared. They exposed us to a diverse array of role models (mostly good and a few bad) and had the courage to ultimately let us make our own choices. They empowered and supported our teachers to correct our self defeating behaviors soon after they occurred, nearly always in private unless a public lesson was a teachable moment.

Be joyful: Whenever I would call Grandpa on the phone during my youth, he was always glad to hear from me. He was fascinated by new ideas. Even as the years slowed him down, he was always able to find a mother lode of silver lining surrounding every cloud. My own children report the same phenomenon when they call Dad.

Be present and be who you are: My father harbors a not-so-secret regret. He attacked the other things on this list with such intensity that he feels he was not present enough in our lives. I disagree. There was never a key question I had that he didn't patiently answer. There was never a major event in my life that he didn't attend, and whenever and wherever he was, he always responded to my phone calls. In those times of rebellion that inevitably touch each generation, he was patient when he needed to be, firm when he had to be and was always true to his beliefs, even when they were not popular.

Ponder this list. How does it parallel some of the other success traits we have been discussing?

As you think about your relationship with the father figures in your life, how many of these dimensions define them?

What if very few do?

I recently had an interesting conversation with a young woman. Her father is what some might describe as her "sperm donor." His own challenges made it hard for him to be the dad she desperately wanted him to be. Despite this, she has grown into a caring, contributing, joyful and complex woman. I encouraged her to remember that he did at least one thing right, because the world is a better place with her in it.

It wouldn't have happened with out him.

The New Normal

"Every time I find the meaning of life, they change it"

Friday at 1:47PM, we heard the words we had been hoping for for the past six months. Dr. Reynolds smiled and said to Colleen, "You are cancer free." The roller coaster ride began in Just after Thanksgiving when our Albuquerque Doctor told The Queen that despite all of our proactivity, the same thing that took her mother and sister from us was now part of our lives.

In addition, I was in the midst of a new opportunity that would relocate us 1,300 miles from New Mexico to a temporary home that would hold us over until we found our next temporary home that would serve us until we selected a "permanent" residence, our 13th house in 32 years of marriage.

To say that the last six months has been a constant exercise in change management is a gross understatement. At this moment it is all good. Colleen is stepping back on the track toward her passions and I am definitely living mine every day.

This is the new normal.

Albert Camus statement that, "Nobody realizes that some people expend tremendous energy merely to be normal," has been the story of our recent life.

But looking back over our long adventure together, there has been no normal, only brief respites from continual change.

How about you? Life is fired at us point-blank. Each day is another story-problem. We are thrust into a constantly evolving arena and must play the game.

I'm reminded of Andrew Bernstein's maxim that, "Nothing is given to us on earth – struggle is built into the nature of life. The hero is the person who lets no obstacle prevent her from pursuing the values she has chosen."

Over 100 different people contributed to WikiHow.com's survival manual on how to cope with whatever your "new normal" may be. I've added my own twist to their thoughts.

- **Be optimistic:** In the 1970s, researchers followed people who had won the lottery and found that a year after they had hit the jackpot, they were no happier than the people who didn't. They called it hedonic adaptation, which suggests that we each have a baseline level of happiness. No matter what happens, good or bad, the effect on our happiness is only temporary and we tend to rebound to our baseline level. Some people have a higher baseline happiness level than others. But it is also largely influenced by how you think. So improving your attitude towards life will increase your happiness permanently.
- **Follow your gut:** In one study, two groups of people were asked to pick out a poster to take home. One group was asked to analyze their decision carefully, weighing the pros and cons, and the other group was told to listen to their gut. Two weeks later, the group that followed their gut was more satisfied with their posters than the group that analyzed their decisions. This does not mean you avoid due diligence on the important turning points in your life. Plug the objective factors into your conscious brain and then allow your subconscious to make the final call.
- **Focus on the basics:** Maslow's Hierarchy of Needs tells us that once you earn enough to support the basics, your

overall quality of life is not significantly affected by how much money you make, but by your level of optimism. And remember, your comfort may increase with your salary, but comfort isn't what makes people happy. It makes people bored. That is why it is important to push beyond your comfort zone to fuel your growth as a person.

- **Stay close to the important people in your life:** Relationships with our friends and family have a far greater impact on our lives than our jobs do. A major part of the joy we feel being back in Michigan is being close, again, to our best friends. So next time you think about relocating factor in the opportunity cost you'll pay by being away from people you love.

- **Find fulfillment in the job you have now:** Many people expect the right job or the right career to dramatically change their level of happiness, but research makes it clear that your level of optimism and the quality of your relationships eclipse the satisfaction you gain from your job. If you have a positive outlook, you will make the best of any job, and if you have good relationships with people, you won't depend on your job to give your life a greater sense of meaning.

- **Smile:** Science suggests that when you smile, whether you feel good or not, your mood will be elevated. So smile all the time! Look for opportunities to praise others and take note of the little things around you that make make the world beautiful.

- **Get a friend / Be a Friend:** Nothing beats talking with someone who is a good listener and who genuinely cares about you. We've written before about the power of giving. Be that friend you would like to have. Be a philanthropist. Give a little of your time, talent and treasure to something you care about.

Like Buckaroo Banzai says, "Wherever you go, there you are." Whatever your new normal is today, dive in and make the most of it.

The Wind Beneath My Wings

"If I had a single flower for every time I think about you,
I could walk forever in my garden."

It feels like yesterday.

It was a Sunday in August when we met, Steve Schram's birthday. Laurie was already in his life and I was happy to sub for him at WVIC so that they could celebrate.

I was a Spartan, working my way through Michigan State University as the utility guy at the station. That meant I helped John Hanley on engineering projects, did a lot of commercial production and filled in for whomever had the day off, while holding down evening shifts on the weekends.

She was still in high school, although you wouldn't have known it by the way she was dressed. Her sense of fashion and her maturity fooled me when she came to the back entrance of our Mount Hope Road studios with a public service announcement.

I was instantly smitten.

Because of our five year age difference, we courted the old fashioned way, under her parents supervision. I was nervous about the chronological gulf between us, but the Aldrichs were many and there were other kids my age. Colleen's dad was a self-made inspiration and her mother was a great cook. That last fact wore me down and I soon found myself eating often at 9335 Warner Road.

We were married on September 23, 1978 at People's Church in East Lansing. The guest list for the reception was something like 150, but the word got out and over 300 showed up. Every disk jockey in town took turns at the microphone and the Haslett High football team served as bouncers.

Thus began a partnership that's now in it's fourth decade.

I got an email the other day from a recently married woman asking what to expect from the institution of marriage. These things happen when your hair starts to turn gray and you have put a significant number of years on the relationship board. I pondered her question and came up with an incomplete definition of a productive marriage.

- Its a union of two people who love and respect each other and continually build one another's self esteem.
- Its a partnership of individuals who have something in common, besides a baby.
- Its a team where there may be some strife and disagreement, but the majority of the time is joyful.
- Its an environment where you live your own lives but can't wait to be together.
- Its two unique and valuable human beings who still work toward their own life goals and continue to retain their individuality.
- Its a relationship where you keep doing the things that attracted you to one another in the first place, because you want to.
- Its a situation where you nearly always feel like you are happier than you were when you were single.

I am sure I have missed some important points, but if focus is on those seven, it is a pretty good start.

Relationships are hard work. The people in them inevitably grow and change. You are continually re-negotiating the rules of engagement, so candid communication helps, too.

But it is worth the effort if you have the right partner.

I can not begin to describe the depth of my love and respect for Colleen. Her singularity of focus on raising our family produced two wonderful children who became even more wonderful adults. She is the best friend a person could have, always the first to call and check in, ever ready to provide moral support, even if the person on the other end might have disappeared from her radar screen for a decade.

Every boss who has met Colleen has told me that she is my best career asset. She exemplifies the down-to-earth, gregarious first-lady that customers and team members instantly love. "The company can do without you," my boss Ron Hartman once said, "but I'd never fire Colleen."

Knowing she and I will be together at the end of the day helps push me through the bad ones, and helps me conclude the good ones on-time. She encourages me to dream big, puts me back on my feet when I fall, and reassures me that we can handle any challenge, as long as we're together.

All my team members know that Wednesday has been our date night for 33 years, a time to continue to practice those things that helped us fall in love in the first place. We send each other morning, noon and night cards on special occasions. And we look forward to the two most important moments of each day: the smiles we exchange when we wake and the "I love yous" we say right before we drop of to sleep.

I love how she continues to grow and wants to learn from life's twists and turns. She's worked in a deli, a shoe store, a boutique, at credit unions, and in a hospital emergency room. When the kids went to college, she focused on her fitness goals. It is a passion that lead her to become a personal trainer who has helped countless others know the joys of health and self esteem.

Through it all, she has been my confidant, my soul mate, my best friend, my accountability buddy. She has followed me across the country to a dozen different assignments and set up shop with courage and enthusiasm at every stop. Her sense of humor still cracks me up, her temper can still strike down a grizzly bear, and her faith that the next day can be better than the last is unshakable, even when terrifying events stare her straight in the face.

It seems to me that life is more fun when you have a partner to share it with. My adult life has been infinitely richer with her by my side. Imperfect for sure. We are an imperfect race. But I'll gladly compare my "smiles-per-hour" ratio with anybody, and it's all because of Colleen.

She had a big birthday today. She wouldn't want me to tell which one it was. But it made me think again about how lucky I was that August day 33 years ago when she walked into my life.

And ever since... She has been the wind beneath my wings.

The Power of One

"The power of one man or one woman doing the right thing
for the right reason, and at the right time,
is the greatest influence in our society." – Jack Kemp

There are moments when you may feel like your contribution to the world is insignificant. This is especially true when fear, temporary failure or a series of setbacks bang away at your attitude.

In those moments, remember the Power of One.

Elton Mayo wrote, "One friend, one person who is truly understanding, who takes the trouble to listen to us as we consider our problems, can change our whole outlook on the work."

Be that person.

Margaret Mead said, "Never underestimate the power of a small group of people to change the world. In fact, it is the only way it ever has." Each of those small groups had one person who inspired them.

Be that person.

On my office wall is a picture of Dr. Martin Luther King, Jr. with his quote, "Almost always, the creative dedicated minority has made the world better." Every generation thirsts for a person with Dr. King's, love, dedication, intellect and tenacity.

Be that person.

This Stephen Covey nugget always re-energizes me: "...one person can be a change catalyst, a 'transformer' in any situation, any organization. Such an individual is yeast that can leaven an entire loaf."

Be that person.

- One person can trigger a million thoughts.
- One person can help you sing the song in your heart when you have forgotten the words
- One dedicated person is worth a hundred who are only interested.
- One person can envision a bridge, an aircraft, a poem, an idea, an atom.
- One person who changes her attitude, can influence the attitudes of all around her.
- One person who treats another as the person he might become will help him become so.
- One person who renders great service inevitably ensures greatness for themselves.

Why not you? Why not now?

- You have already changed at least one person's life for the better.
- You have already done at least one thing exceptionally well.
- You are already admired by someone.
- You have an idea floating around in your head right now that could change the world.

Whatever your do, wherever you are, you can harness The Power of One.

Don't expect to find life worth living; make it that way.

Acknowledgments

Brandon Westerman, for finding something to praise in everything I write. Shelby Westerman, for the inspiration when I needed it. And Stephanie Westerman, for photography that makes a grey haired guy look better than he should.

Jennifer Decker, for organizing my life so I had room for this project.

Susan Whitall, Lynn Henning and Andru Reeve, for showing me how it's done.

W. Scott Westerman, Jr., the "Real" Scott Westerman, for a lifetime of being my role model and example. I want to grow up to be just like you, Dad!

Alan and Salem. You guys never met, but I'm certain you are brothers.

Tiare Romero and Diane Villegas, for surpassing everybody's expectations, except mine. I knew you could do it, all along.

Chris Dunkeson, for taking that different seat on the bus.

Jeff Smith, for 37 years of friendship and guidance.

Steve Schram, for pointing me toward the job of a lifetime.

Bob Groves, for giving me the job of a lifetime.

Brad Dusto, for giving me the job of a lifetime.

Jeff Delorme, for giving me the job of a lifetime.

Bob Green, for making me feel like I really was one of the Keener guys. And Bob Berry, for showing us that there still are Keener guys out there.

Elizabeth Battiste, who knows that making the world better is the best revenge.

Josanna Sutka, who got me running again.

Ryan Schram, Leigh Graves Wolf, Megan Gebhart and a score of other young Spartans, who give me faith in the future.

Tracy Lee Carroll for turning my verbal prose into something readable.

And Colleen Yvonne Aldrich Westerman, the most courageous woman I know. For a man who can find words for any occasion, none come close to describing how much I love you.

Suggested Reading

Delivering Happiness – Tony Hsieh
The Difference Maker – John C. Maxwell
The Eighth Habit - Stephen Covey
The Element – Ken Robinson
Feel the Fear and Do It Anyway – Susan Jeffers
Good to Great / How the Mighty Fall - Jim Collins
How to Get Control of Your Time and Your Life - Alan Lakein
Influencer: The Power to Change Anything – Kerry Patterson
In Love and War – James B. Stockdale / Sybil Stockdale
Laws of Success – Napoleon Hill
Leading With Soul – Bolman & Deal
Lynchpin - Seth Godin
Made to Stick – Chip Heath
Man's Search for Meaning – Vicktor Frankl
Never Eat Alone / Who's Got Your Back - Keith Ferrazzi
The Power of Feedback - Joseph R. Folkman
The Power of Positive Thinking – Norman Vincent Peale
The Psychology of Winning – Denis Waitley
The Secret Language of Leadership – Stephen Denning
The Servant as Leader - Robert K. Greenleaf
Tribal Leadership – Dave Logan
Twelve Pillars – Jim Rohn
The Ultimate Question – Fred Reicheld

Websites

ScottWesterman.com
alumni.msu.edu

About the Author

Scott Westerman's 40 year tele-communications career spans every corner of the industry.

As a broadcaster, cable television executive and entrepreneur, he has been involved in business start-ups, corporate acquisitions, and process improvement activities in a wide array of organizations.

After a 17 year association with Continental Cablevision and its successor, MediaOne, Westerman developed and launched a series of businesses, from international broadcasting, to an Internet start-up, to aviation leasing.

During his career in cable telecommunications, he built and operated cable communications systems in ten states, and was among the first in the industry to deploy pay-per-view, high speed Internet, business to business data services and telephony.

He was a principal in the World Beacon international radio network and his technical process design for program content distribution has been implemented by the British Broadcasting Corporation.

In 1999 he co-founded the Emergency Email Network which utilizes a patent pending delivery process to disseminate critical disaster information for the National Weather Service, the US Geological Survey, and other government and corporate clients.

He was an early pioneer of podcasting and social media, contributing to Comcast's groundbreaking Twitter customer care strategy and co-founding The Spartan Podcast at Michigan State University. His interests include renewable energy where he was an early adopter of alternative fuel technology, driving a diesel vehicle he converted to run on recycled vegetable oil.

Westerman is a 1978 graduate of Michigan State University. He is a 2001 distinguished alumnus of the College of Communications Arts and Sciences where he and his wife established the Scott & Colleen Westerman Technology Endowment.

After serving as a local club officer in several states, a volunteer, lecturer and national MSU alumni board member, he joined the University in January of 2010 as Associate Vice President for Alumni Relations and Executive Director of the MSU Alumni Association.

He and his wife, Colleen have four grown children and a legion of "adopted" kids across the country.

Also by Scott Westerman:

Touch and Go - A Story of Flight
order via ScottWesterman.com

The "Block S" is a registered trademark of Michigan State University. This is an independent publication and has not been authorized, sponsored or approved by Michigan State University.

Cover photo by Peter Delong.
Cover design by Brandon Westerman.